Street Atlas
BOURN

C000133285

CONTENTS

REFERENCE

A Road	A35	Posttown Boundary By arrangement with the Post Office	
Under Construction		Postcode Boundary Within Posttowns	
Proposed		Map Continuation	12
B Road	B3064		
Dual Carriageway		Ambulance Station	✚
One Way Street Traffic flow on A Roads is indicated by a heavy line on the driver's left.	→	Car Park Selected	P
		Church or Chapel	†
Pedestrianized Road		Fire Station	■
Restricted Access		Hospital	H
Footpath		House Numbers Selected Roads	83 96
Residential Walkway		Information Centre	i
Railway	Level Crossing / Station	National Grid Reference	¹10
County or Unitary Authority Boundary		Police Station	▲
District Boundary		Post Office	★
Built Up Area	MILL ST.	Toilet With facilities for the Disabled	▽ ♿

SCALE

4 inches to 1 mile

0 ... ¼ ... ½ ... ¾ mile

0 ... 250 ... 500 ... 750 ... 1 kilometre

1:15,840

Geographers' A-Z Map Company Ltd.

Head Office:
Fairfield Road, Borough Green, Sevenoaks, Kent, TN15 8PP
Telephone 01732 781000

Showrooms:
44 Gray's Inn Road, London, WC1X 8HX
Telephone 0171 242 9246

The Maps in the Atlas are based upon the Ordnance Survey 1:10,560 Maps with the permission of the Controller of Her Majesty's Stationery Office. © Crown Copyright.

Every possible care has been taken to ensure that the information given in this publication is accurate and whilst the publishers would be grateful to learn of any errors, they regret they cannot accept any responsibility for loss thereby caused.

© Edition 3 1995   Copyright of the Publishers

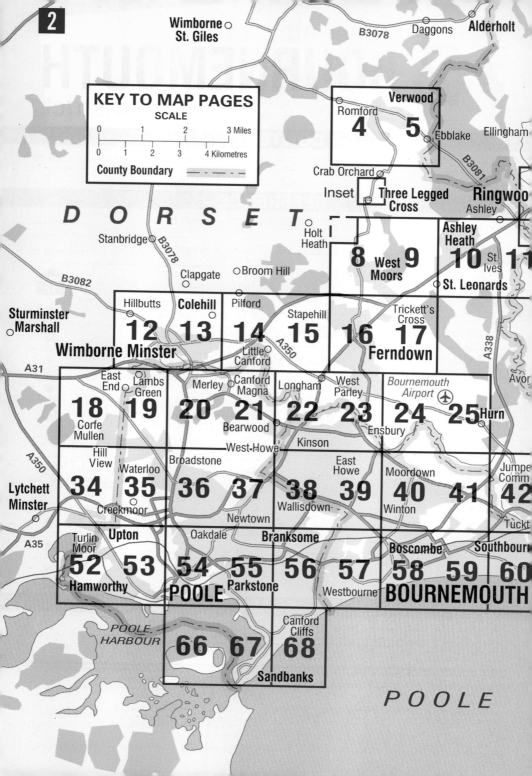

2

KEY TO MAP PAGES

SCALE

0   1   2   3 Miles

0   1   2   3   4 Kilometres

County Boundary ––·––·––

Wimborne St. Giles

B3078   Daggons   **Alderholt**

Verwood

Romford

4   **5**   Ebblake   Ellingham

B3081

Crab Orchard

Inset   **Three Legged Cross**   **Ringwoo**

Ashley

D O R S E T

Stanbridge   B3078

Holt Heath

Ashley Heath

B3082   Clapgate   Broom Hill

8   **West Moors**   **9**   **10**   St. Ives   **11**

St. Leonards

Sturminster Marshall

Hillbutts   **Colehill**   Pilford   Stapehill   Trickett's Cross

12   **13**   **14**   **15**   **16**   **17**

Wimborne Minster   Little Canford   A350   **Ferndown**

A31

East End   Lambs Green   Merley   Canford Magna   Longham   West Parley   *Bournemouth Airport*   A338   Avo

18   **19**   **20**   **21**   **22**   **23**   **24**   **25** Hurn

Corfe Mullen   Bearwood   Ensbury

West Howe   Kinson

Hill View   Waterloo   Broadstone   East Howe   Moordown   Jumpe Comm

A350

Lytchett Minster

34   **35**   **36**   **37**   **38**   **39**   **40**   **41**   **42**

Creekmoor   Newtown   Wallisdown   Winton   Tuck

A35

Turlin Moor   **Upton**   Oakdale   **Branksome**   **Boscombe**   **Southbour**

52   **53**   **54**   **55**   **56**   **57**   **58**   **59**   **60**

Hamworthy   **POOLE**   **Parkstone**   Westbourne   **BOURNEMOUTH**

POOLE HARBOUR

Canford Cliffs

66   **67**   **68**

Sandbanks

P O O L E

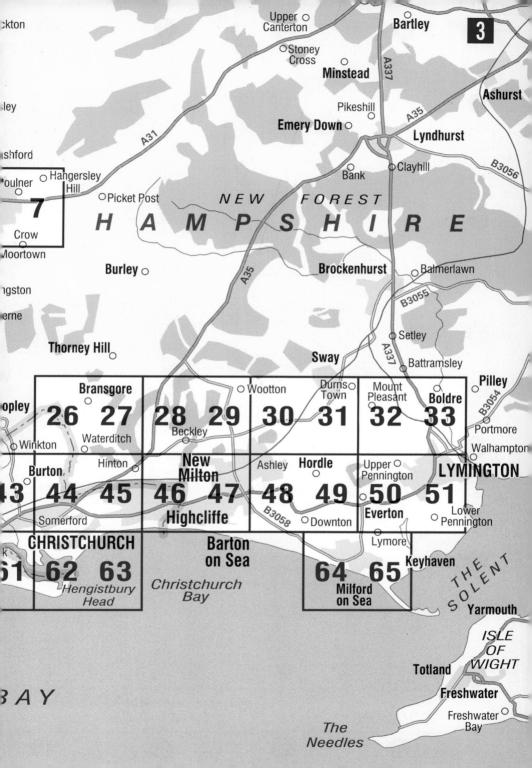

3

Upper Canterton
Bartley
Stoney Cross
Minstead
Ashurst
A337
Pikeshill
A35
Emery Down
Lyndhurst
B3056
Bank
Clayhill
ley
shford
Hangersley Hill
Picket Post
NEW FOREST
7
HAMPSHIRE
oulner
Crow
Moortown
Burley
Brockenhurst
Balmerlawn
A35
B3055
ngston
erne
Setley
Thorney Hill
Sway
A337
Battramsley
Pilley
B3054
Bransgore
Wootton
Durns Town
Mount Pleasant
Boldre
opley
26 **27**
28 **29**
30 **31**
32 **33**
Portmore
Winkton
Waterditch
Beckley
Walhampton
Burton
Hinton
New Milton
Ashley
Hordle
Upper Pennington
LYMINGTON
43 **44** **45**
46 **47**
48 **49**
50 **51**
Somerford
Highcliffe
B3058
Downton
Everton
Lower Pennington
CHRISTCHURCH
Barton on Sea
Lymore
Keyhaven
61 **62** **63**
64 **65**
THE SOLENT
Hengistbury Head
Christchurch Bay
Milford on Sea
Yarmouth
ISLE OF WIGHT
Totland
Freshwater
BAY
The Needles
Freshwater Bay

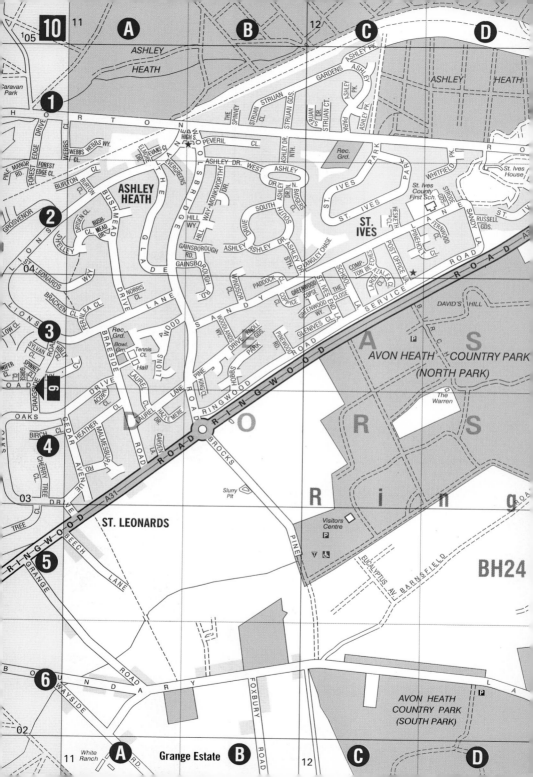

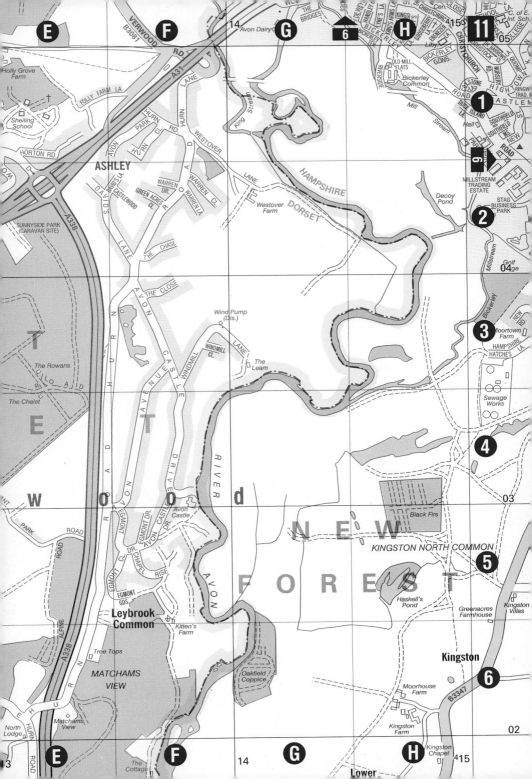

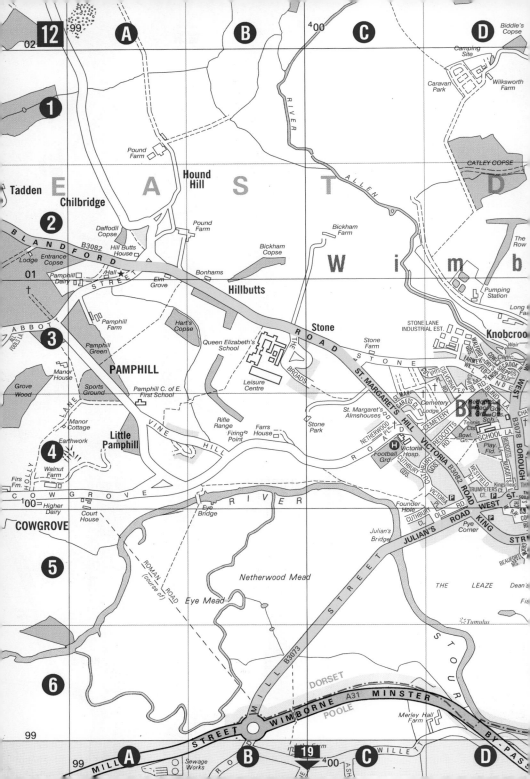

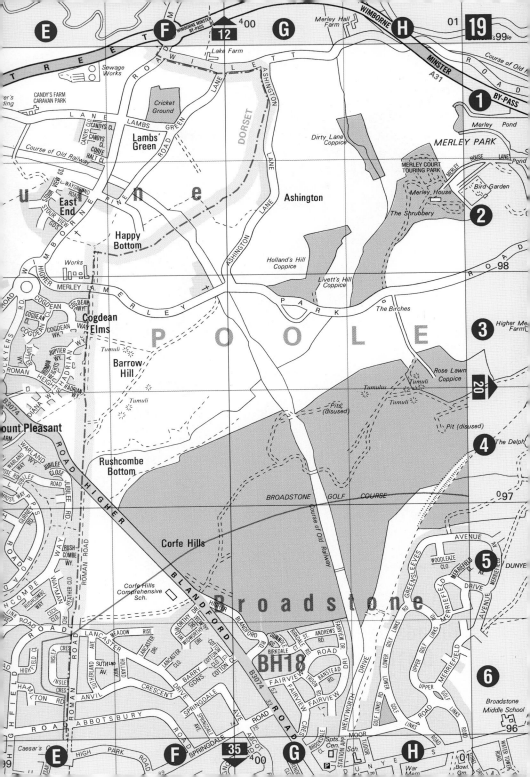

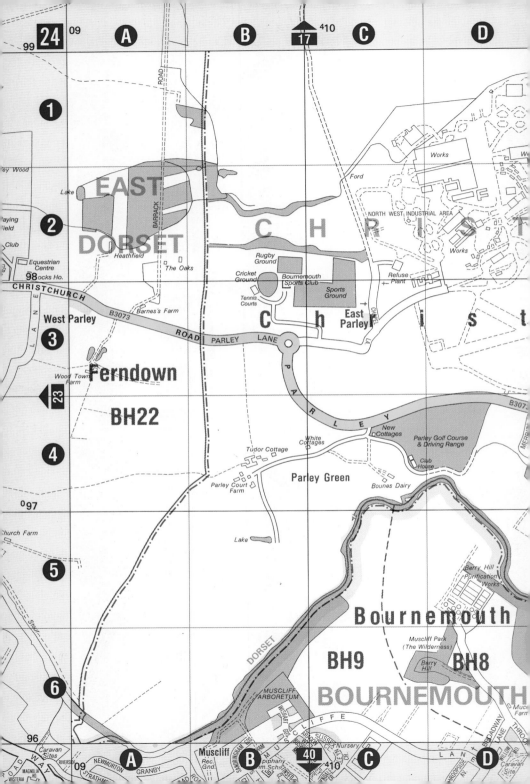

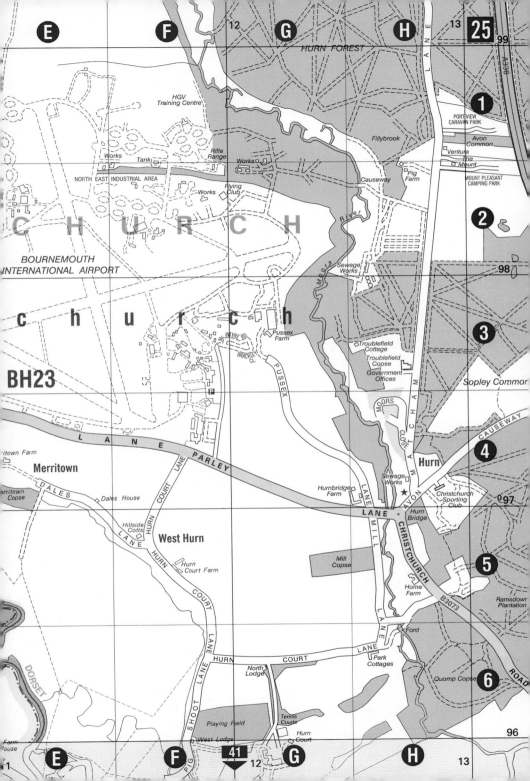

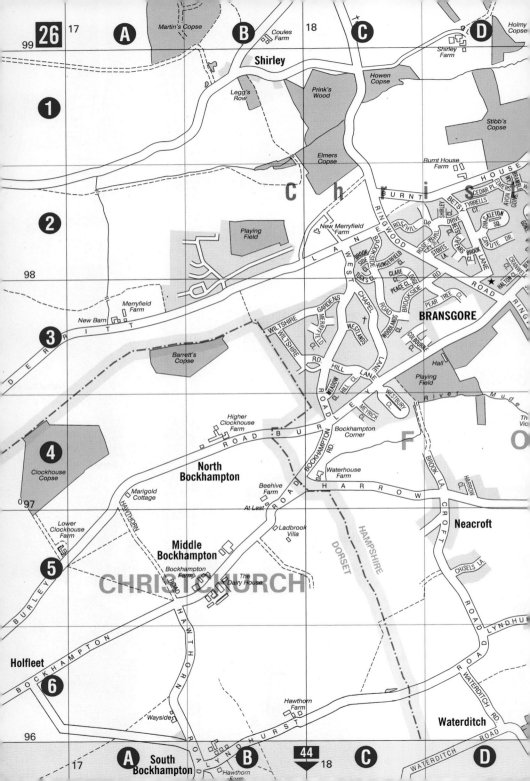

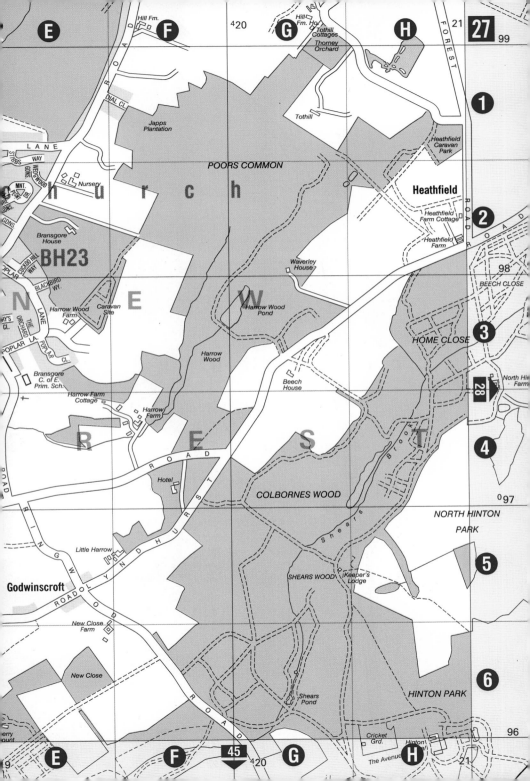

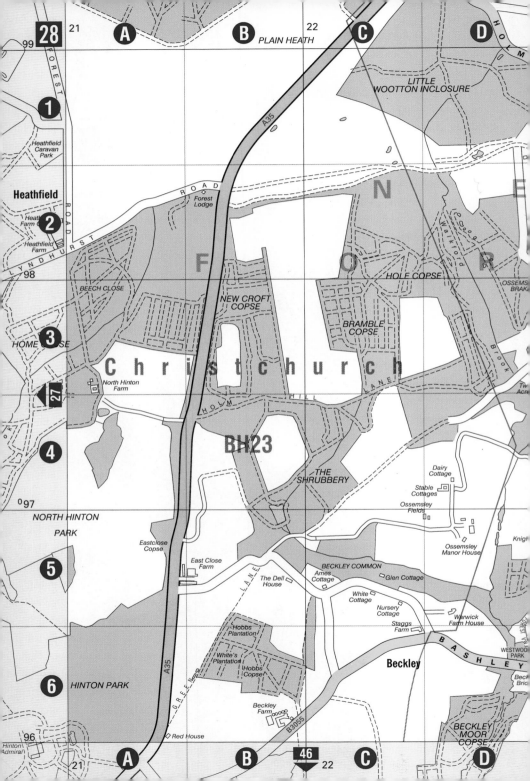

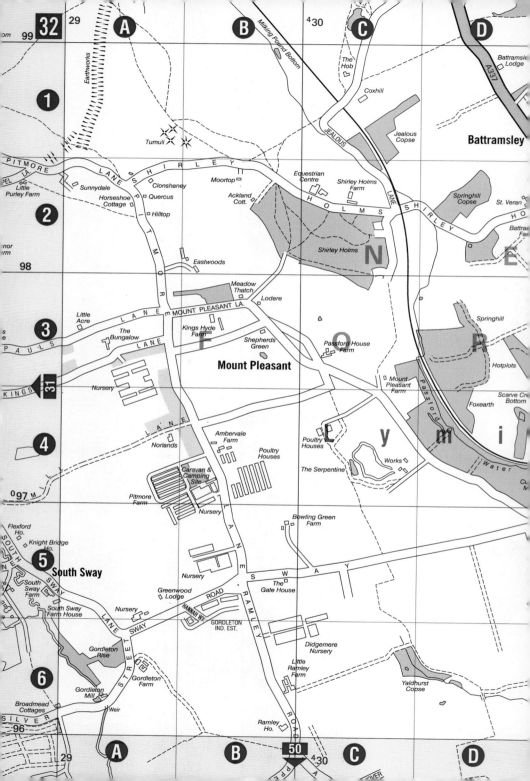

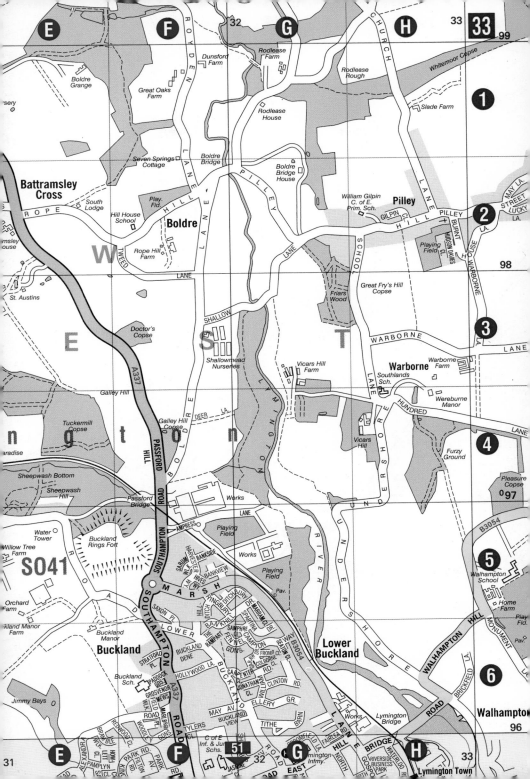

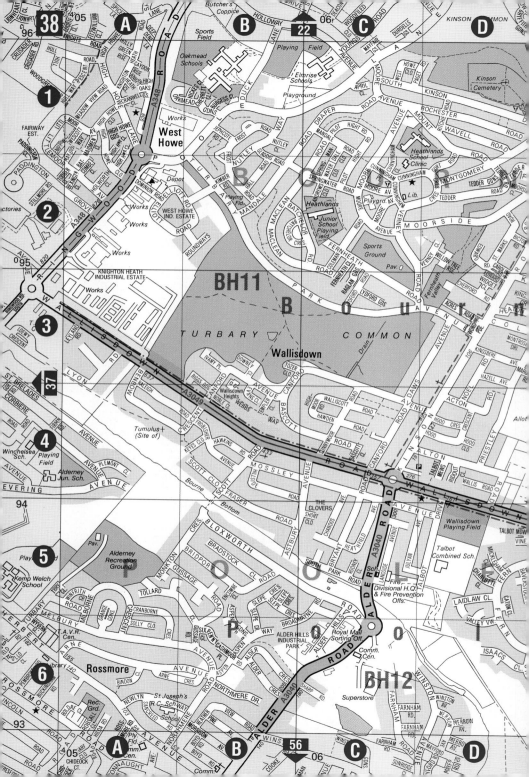

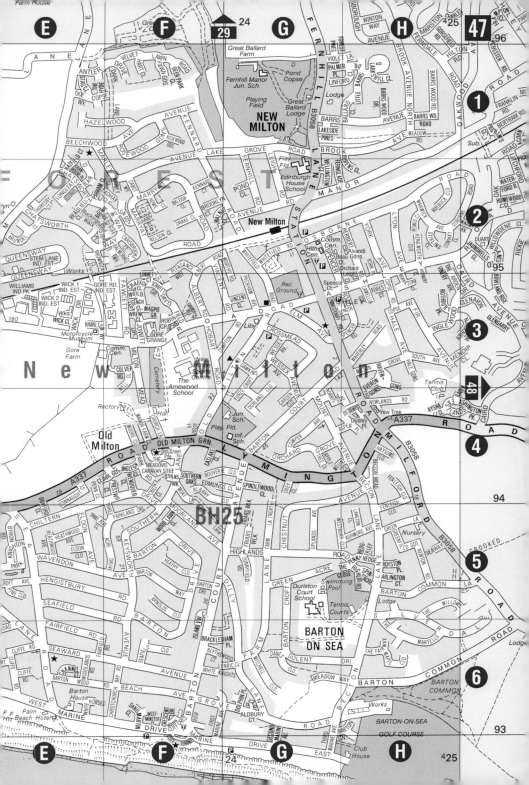

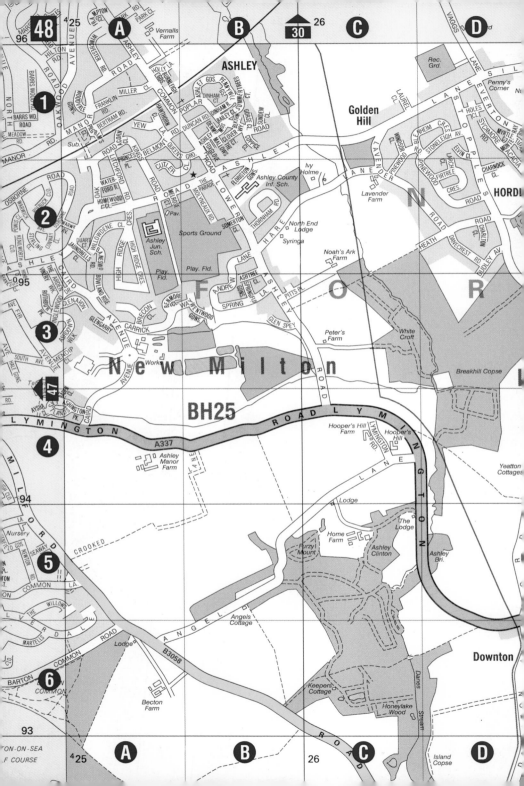

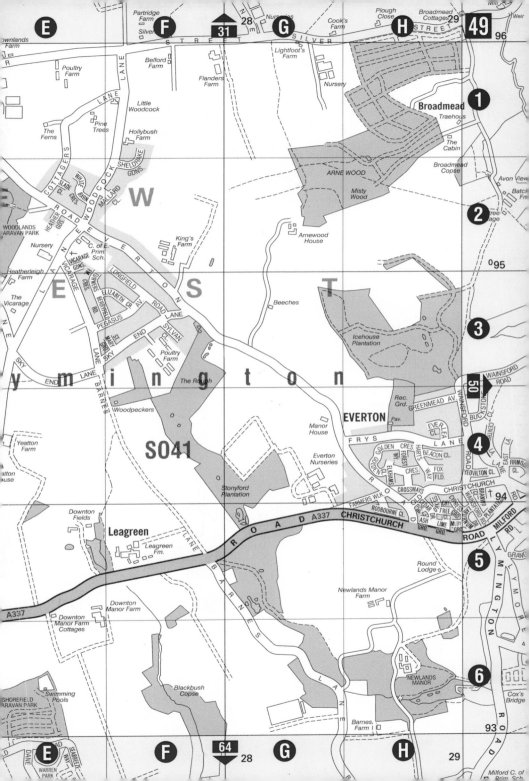

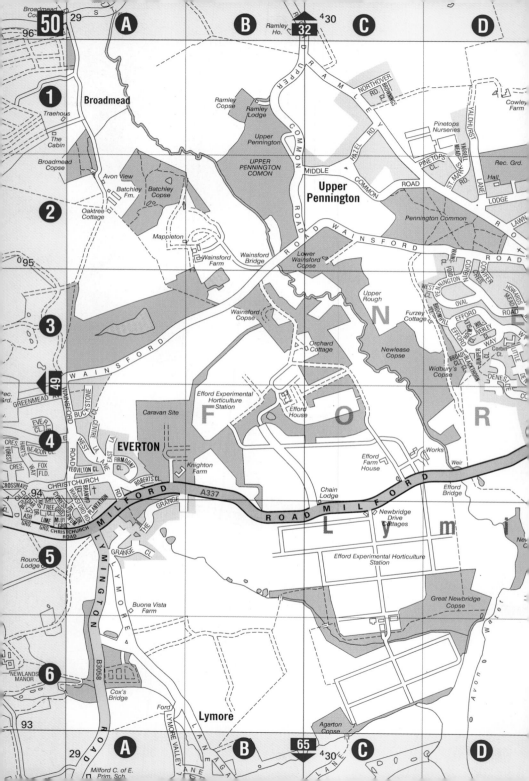

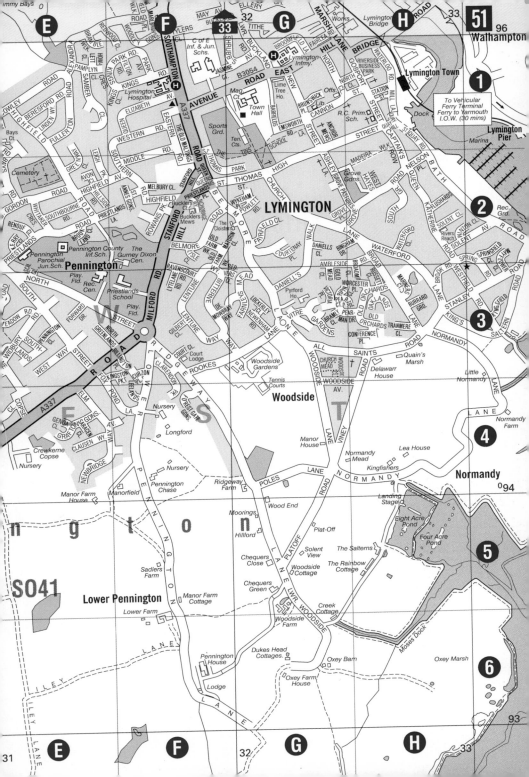

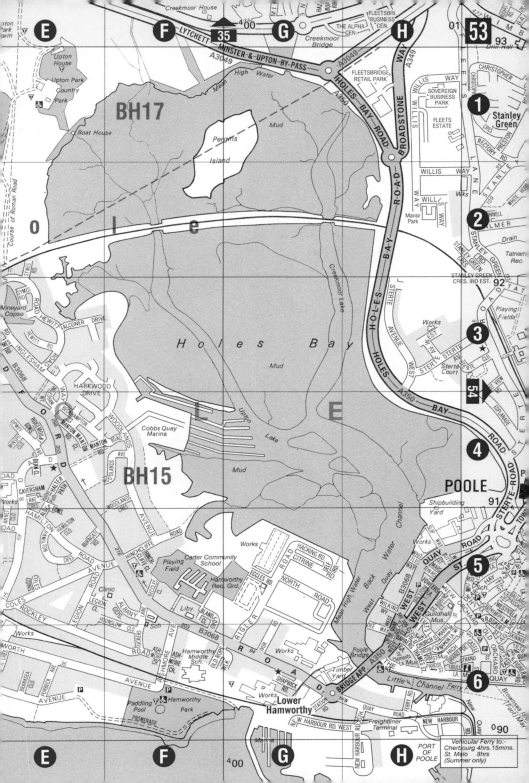

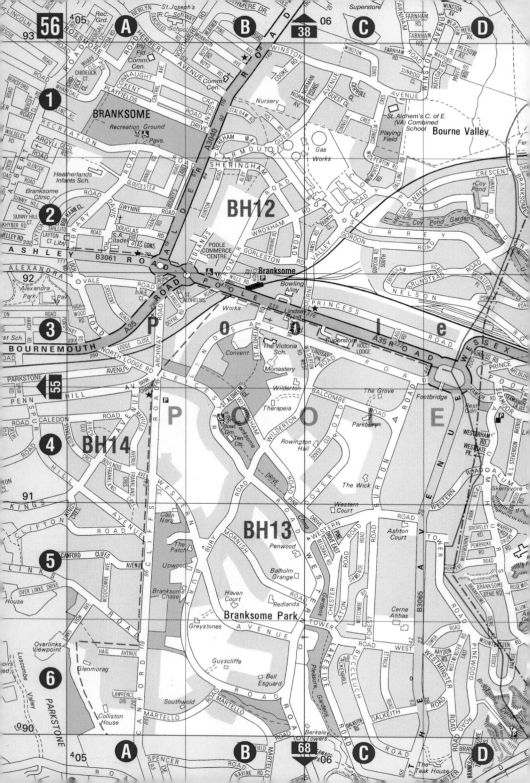

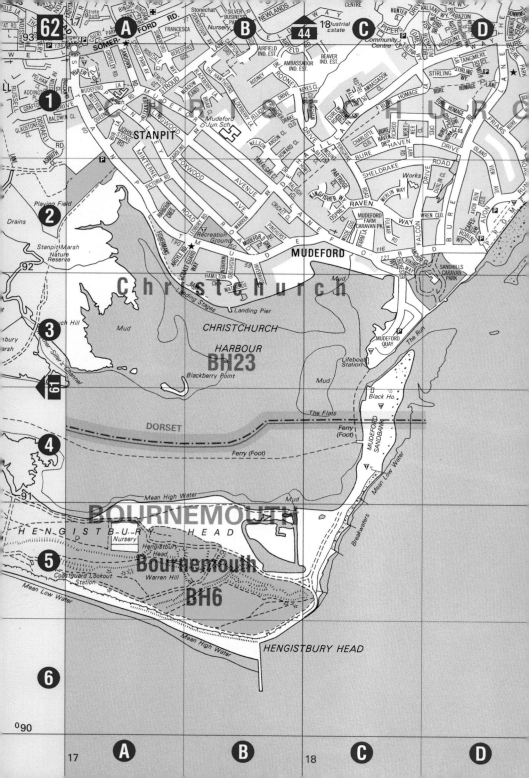

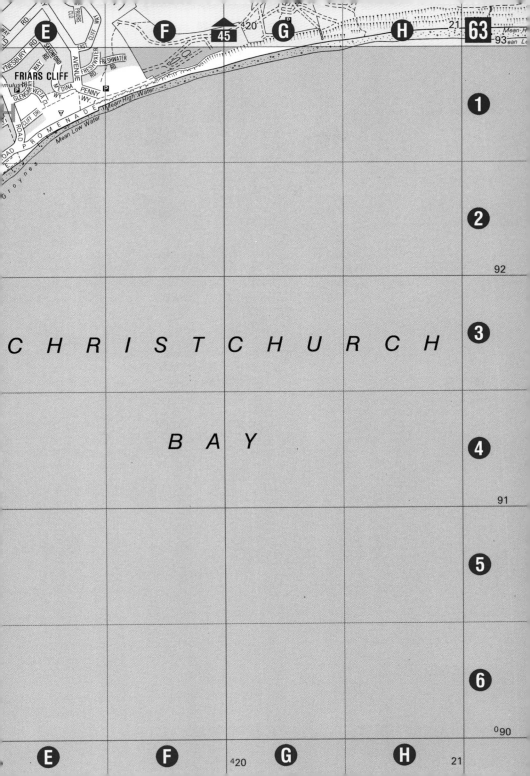

E **F** **45** **20** **G** **H** 21 93 Mean H ean L

FRIARS CLIFF

YNESBURY RD
SAXONFORD RD
EAST CLIFF WAY
FRESHWATER
FRESHWATER RD
AVENUE
MEDINA
PENNY
GLENGARRY RD
CLIFF DR
CLIFF
RD
PROMENADE
ROAD
Mean High Water
Mean Low Water
Groynes
ROAD
PRIORS
CLD

1

2

92

C H R I S T C H U R C H

3

B A Y

4

91

5

6

0 90

E **F** 4 20 **G** **H** 21

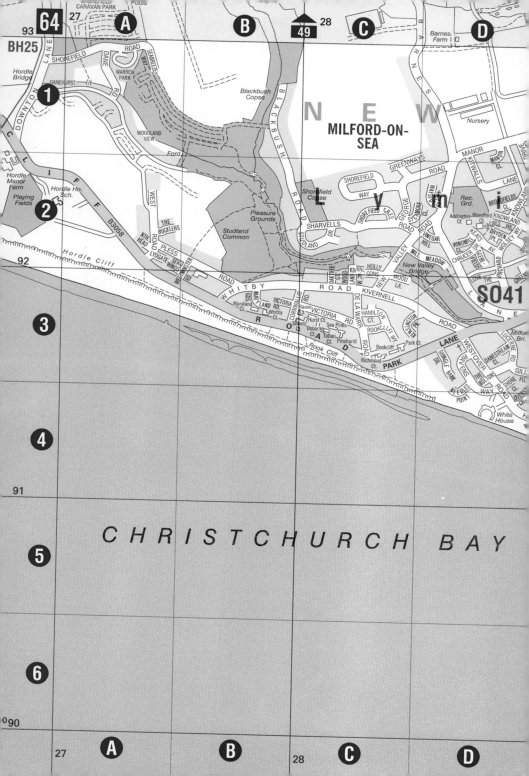

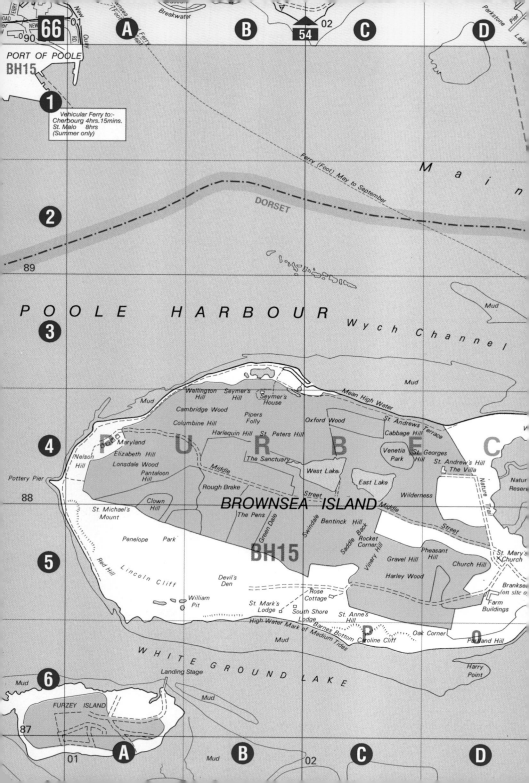

INDEX TO STREETS

HOW TO USE THIS INDEX

1. Each street name is followed by its Posttown or Postal Locality, and then by its map reference: e.g. Abbey Rd. W Moor —1E **17** is in the West Moors Postal Locality an is to be found in square 1E on page **17**; the page number being shown in bold type.
A strict alphabetical order.is followed in which Av., Rd., St., etc. (though abbreviated) are read in full and as part of the street name; e.g. Abbotts Way appears after Abbott St. but before Aberdare Rd.

2. Streets and a selection of Subsidiary names not shown on the Maps, appear in the index in *Italics* with the thoroughfare to which it is connected shown in brackets; e.g. *Acorns, The. Fern —1F* **17** (off Oak Tree Farm Caravan Pk.)

GENERAL ABBREVIATIONS

All : Alley
App : Approach
Arc : Arcade
Av : Avenue
Bk : Back
Boulevd :· Boulevard
Bri : Bridge
B'way : Broadway
Bldgs : Buildings
Bus : Business
Cen : Centre
Chu : Church
Chyd : Churchyard
Circ : Circle
Cir : Circus

Clo : Close
Comn : Common
Cotts : Cottages
Ct : Court
Cres : Crescent
Dri : Drive
E : East
Embkmt : Embankment
Est : Estate
Gdns : Gardens
Ga : Gate
Gt : Great
Grn : Green
Gro : Grove
Ho : House

Ind : Industrial
Junct : Junction
La : Lane
Lit : Little
Lwr : Lower
Mnr : Manor
Mans : Mansions
Mkt : Market
M : Mews
Mt : Mount
N : North
Pal : Palace
Pde : Parade
Pk : Park
Pas : Passage

Pl : Place
Rd : Road
S : South
Sq : Square
Sta : Station
St : Street
Ter : Terrace
Up : Upper
Vs : Villas
Wlk : Walk
W : West
Yd : Yard

POSTTOWN AND POSTAL LOCALITY ABBREVIATIONS

Ashtn : Ashington
Ashy : Ashley
Ashy H : Ashley Heath
Bcn H : Beacon Hill
Blash : Blashford
Bock : Bockhampton
Bold : Boldre
Bosc : Boscombe
Bourn : Bournemouth
Brnk : Branksome
Brnk P : Branksome Park
Brans : Bransgore
Broad : Broadstone
Burt : Burton
Can C : Canford Cliffs
Christ : Christchurch

Cole : Colehill
Cor M. Corfe Mullen
Cowg : Cowgrove
Crow : Crow
Down : Downton
Evtn : Everton
Fern : Ferndown
Ham : Hamworthy
Hang : Hangersley
High : Hightown
High H : Hightown Hill
Hint : Hinton
Hord : Hordle
Hurn : Hurn
Key : Keyhaven
Lym : Lymington

Ly Min : Lytchett Minster
Mil S : Milford on Sea
New M : New Milton
N'brne : Northbourne
Oak : Oakdale
Oss : Ossemsley
Pamp : Pamphill
Park : Parkstone
Parl : Parley
Penn : Pennington
Pill : Pilley
Poole : Poole
P'mre : Portmore
Poul : Poulner
Ring : Ringwood
St I : St Ives

St L : St Leonards
S'brne : Southbourne
Sway : Sway
Thor H : Thorney Hill
T Leg : Three Legged Cross
Tip : Tiptoe
Uptn : Upton
Ver : Verwood
Walf : Walford
Wal : Walhampton
Walk : Walkford
Wat : Waterloo
W Moor : West Moors
W Parl : West Parley
Wim : Wimborne
Wink : Winkton

INDEX TO STREETS

Aaron Clo. Poole —6D **36**
Abbey Gdns. Wim —4D **14**
Abbey Rd. W Moor —1E **17**
Abbotsbury Rd. Broad —6E **19**
Abbots Clo. Christ —5H **45**
Abbott Rd. Bourn —5A **40**
Abbott St. Pamp —3A **12**
Abbotts Way. W Moor —1E **17**
Aberdare Rd. Bourn —2G **39**
Abingdon Dri. Christ —5C **46**
Abingdon Rd. Poole —5B **36**
Abinger Rd. Bourn —1G **59**
Abney Rd. Bourn —2F **39**
Acacia Av. Ver —5G **5**
Acacia Rd. Hord —1D **48**
Acland Rd. Bourn —5B **40**
Acorn Clo. Christ —5D **42**
Acorn Clo. New M —1A **48**
Acorn Clo. St L —4A **10**
Acorns, The. Wim —5A **14**
Acres Rd. Bourn —3D **38**
Acton Rd. Bourn —4D **38**
Adamsfield Gdns. Bourn —3E **39**
Adastral Rd. Poole —4C **36**
Adastral Sq. Poole —5D **36**
Addington Ct. Mil S —2D **64**
Addington Pl. Christ —1H **61**
Addiscombe Rd. Christ —6E **43**
Addison Sq. Ring —4D **6**
Adelaide Clo. Christ —5D **42**
Adelaide La. Bourn —4H **57**
Adelaide Rd. Poole —4B **54**
Adeline Rd. Bourn —3E **59**
Adlam's La. Sway —1D **30**

Admirals Wlk. Bourn —5F **57**
Admiralty Rd. Bourn —4D **60**
Agars La. Hord —5E **31**
Agarton La. Mil S —1F **65**
Aggis Farm Rd. Ver —3C **4**
Aireton's Clo. Broad —2A **36**
Airfield Ind. Est. Christ —1B **62**
Airfield Rd. Christ —6B **44**
Airfield Way. Christ —6B **44**
Airspeed Rd. Christ —6D **44**
Akeshill Clo. New M —6H **29**
Alan Ct. Christ —6B **46**
Albany. Bourn —4C **58**
Albany Clo. New M —4F **47**
Albany Dri. T Leg —1A **8**
Albany Gdns. Poole —5F **53**
Albany Pk. Poole —5H **35**
Albemarle Rd. Bourn —6H **39**
Albert Rd. Bourn —4H **57**
Albert Rd. Cor M —6D **18**
Albert Rd. Fern —4A **16**
(in two parts)
Albert Rd. New M —3F **47**
Albert Rd. Poole —2H **55**
Albion Clo. Poole —6F **37**
Albion Rd. Christ —4D **42**
Albion Way. Ver —2B **4**
Alby Rd. Poole —2B **56**
Alcester Rd. Poole —1H **55**
Aldbury Ct. New M —6G **47**
Alder Clo. Burt —4H **43**
Alder Cres. Poole —6B **38**
Alder Hills. Poole —6C **38**
Alder Hills Ind. Pk. Poole —6C **38**
Alderley Rd. Bourn —1F **39**
Alderney Av. Poole —4G **37**

Alder Rd. Poole —2A **56**
Aldis Gdns. Poole —5E **53**
Aldridge Rd. Bourn —1E **39**
Aldridge Rd. Fern —6C **16**
Aldridge Way. Fern —6D **16**
(off Lone Pine Caravan Pk.)
Alexander Clo. Christ —1A **62**
Alexandra Rd. Bourn —2A **60**
Alexandra Rd. Lym —1E **51**
Alexandra Rd. Poole —3G **55**
Alford Rd. Bourn —6F **39**
Alington Clo. Poole —2G **67**
Alington Rd. Bourn —1A **58**
Alington Rd. Poole —2G **67**
Alipore Clo. Poole —4H **55**
Allenby Clo. Poole —3H **35**
Allenby Rd. Poole —4H **35**
Allen Ct. Wim —4E **13**
Allen Rd. Wim —5E **13**
Allens La. Uptn —2D **52**
Allens Rd. Poole —1C **52**
Allenview Rd. Wim —3E **13**
All Fools La. Pamp —3A **12**
All Saints Rd. Lym —3G **51**
Alma Rd. Bourn —6H **39**
Almer Rd. Poole —4E **53**
Almond Gro. Poole —6H **37**
Alpha Cen., The. Poole —6H **35**
Alpine Rd. Ring —6E **11**
Alton Rd. Bourn —4D **38**
Alton Rd. Poole —4F **55**
Alton Rd. E. Poole —4H **55**
Alum Chine Rd. Bourn —4D **56**
Alumdale Rd. Bourn —5D **56**
Alumhurst Rd. Bourn —4D **56**
Alum Promenade. Bourn —6E **57**

Alvandi Gdns. New M —2H **47**
Alverton Av. Poole —4C **54**
Alyth Rd. Bourn —1E **57**
Ambassador Clo. Christ —1C **62**
Ambassador Ind. Est. Christ
—1C **62**
Amberley Clo. Christ —5G **45**
Amber Rd. Cor M —1C **34**
Amberwood. Fern —3C **16**
Amberwood. New M —6C **46**
Amberwood Clo. Christ —3A **46**
Amberwood Dri. Christ —3H **45**
Amberwood Gdns. Christ —3A **46**
Ambleside. Christ —2B **42**
Ambleside Rd. Lym —2G **51**
Ambury La. Christ —5A **44**
Amesbury Rd. Bourn —1A **60**
Amethyst Rd. Christ —6B **44**
Ameysford Rd. Fern —6A **8**
(in two parts)
Ameys La. Fern —2D **16**
Ampfield Rd. Bourn —2D **40**
Ampress La. Lym —5F **33**
Amsterdam Sq. Christ —6H **43**
Anchorage Way. Lym —2F **51**
Anchor Clo. Bourn —6B **22**
Anchor Clo. Christ —2C **62**
Alpha Cen., The. Poole —6H **35**
Anchor M. Lym —1G **51**
Anchor Rd. Bourn —6B **22**
Anderwood Dri. Sway —1F **31**
Andover Clo. Christ —6D **44**
Andrew La. New M —3B **48**
Andrews Clo. Bourn —2C **38**
Angeline Clo. Christ —5H **45**
Angel La. Fern —6H **15**
Angel La. New M —6A **48**

Anne Clo. Christ —4E **43**
Annerley Rd. Bourn —3C **58**
Annet Clo. Poole —5E **53**
Anson Clo. Christ —1B **62**
Anson Rd. Ring —3E **7**
Anstey Clo. Bourn —5C **22**
Anstey Rd. Bourn —6C **22**
Anthony's Av. Poole —1F **67**
Antler Dri. New M —1E **47**
Anvil Cres. Broad —6E **19**
Apollo Clo. Poole —6H **37**
Apple Gro. Christ —3C **42**
Appleslade Way. New M —6H **29**
Appletree Clo. Bourn —2A **60**
Appletree Clo. New M —4G **47**
Apple Tree Gro. Fern —3C **16**
Approach Rd. Poole —4F **55**
April Clo. Bourn —1C **38**
Apsley Cres. Bourn —4H **35**
Aragon Way. Bourn —6B **24**
Arcade, The. Bourn —4H **57**
Arcadia Av. Bourn —6B **40**
Arcadia Rd. Christ —4D **42**
Archdale Clo. Bourn —3F **39**
Archway Rd. Poole —3A **56**
Arden Rd. Bourn —2H **39**
Arden Wlk. New M —3H **47**
Ardmore Rd. Poole —3F **55**
Argyle Rd. Christ —2A **62**
Argyll Rd. Bourn —3E **59**
Argyll Rd. Poole —1H **55**
Ariel Clo. Bourn —3F **61**
Ariel Dri. Bourn —3F **61**
Ark Dri. Fern —6D **16**
  (off Lone Pine Caravan Pk.)
Arley Rd. Poole —5E **55**
Arlington Ct. New M —5H **47**
Arne Av. Poole —6A **38**
Arne Cres. Poole —6A **38**
Arnewood Bri. Rd. Sway —4C **30**
Arnewood Rd. Bourn —3A **60**
Arnold Clo. W Moor —4C **8**
Arnold Rd. W Moor —4C **8**
Arnolds Clo. New M —5F **47**
Arran Way. Christ —4B **46**
Arrowsmith La. Wim —4C **20**
Arrowsmith Rd. Wim —6B **20**
Arthur Clo. Bourn —2H **57**
Arthur La. Christ —6E **43**
Arthur Rd. Christ —6E **43**
Arundel Clo. New M —2E **47**
Arundel Way. Christ —6H **45**
Ascham Rd. Bourn —2B **58**
Ascot Rd. Broad —1G **35**
Ashbourne Rd. Bourn —2H **59**
Ashburton Gdns. Bourn —4F **39**
Ash Clo. Poole —5B **34**
Ashdene Clo. Wim —4F **13**
Ashdown Clo. Poole —4C **36**
Ashdown Wlk. New M —3A **48**
Ashford Rd. Bourn —6B **42**
Ash Gro. Evtn —5H **49**
Ash Gro. Ring —4E **7**
Ashington La. Ashtn —1G **19**
Ashington Pk. New M —4A **48**
Ashlet Gdns. New M —1B **48**
Ashley Clo. Bourn —1E **59**
Ashley Clo. Poole —5F **7**
Ashley Comn. Rd. New M —6A **30**
Ashley Ct. Fern —1E **17**
Ashley Dri. N. Ashy H —2B **10**
  (in three parts)
Ashley Dri. S. Ashy H —2B **10**
Ashley Dri. W. Ashy H —2B **10**
Ashley La. Lym —2G **51**
Ashley La. New M & Hord —2B **48**
Ashley Meadows. New M —1B **48**
Ashley Pk. Ashy H —1C **10**
Ashley Rd. Bourn —1E **59**
Ashley Rd. New M —3G **47**
Ashley Rd. Poole —2F **55**
Ashling Clo. Bourn —5C **40**
Ashling Cres. Bourn —5B **40**
Ashmeads Clo. Wim —3A **14**

Ashmeads Way. Wim —3A **14**
Ashmore. Wim —5F **13**
Ashmore Av. New M —5H **47**
Ashmore Av. Poole —6F **53**
Ashmore Cres. Poole —6F **53**
Ashmore Gro. Christ —4G **45**
Ashridge Av. Bourn —6F **23**
Ashridge Gdns. Bourn —6F **23**
Ashridge Pde. Bourn —6F **23**
Ashton Rd. Bourn —3H **39**
Ashtree Clo. New M —3B **48**
Ashurst Rd. Bourn —2D **40**
Ashurst Rd. W Moor —4B **8**
Ashwood Dri. Broad —1A **36**
Aspen Dri. Ver —3F **5**
Aspen Gdns. Poole —5B **38**
Aspen Pl. New M —4H **47**
Aspen Rd. Poole —6B **38**
Aspen Way. Poole —6B **38**
Asquith Clo. Christ —1H **61**
Astbury Av. Poole —5B **38**
Aston Mead. Christ —1C **42**
Athelstan Rd. Bourn —2C **60**
Aubrey Clo. Mil S —3F **65**
Auckland Rd. Christ —6E **45**
Audemer Ct. Ring —3E **7**
Austen Av. Bourn —5F **23**
Auster Clo. Christ —6D **44**
Austin Av. Poole —6F **55**
Austin Clo. Bourn —2D **58**
Autumn Clo. Fern —2H **15**
Avalon. Poole —1G **67**
Avebury Av. Bourn —5G **23**
Avenue La. Bourn —4G **57**
Avenue Rd. Bourn —4G **57**
Avenue Rd. Christ —6D **42**
Avenue Rd. Lym —1F **51**
Avenue Rd. New M —2G **47**
Avenue Rd. Walk —4C **46**
Avenue Rd. Wim —5F **13**
Avenue Shopping Cen., The. Bourn
  —4G **57**
Avenue, The. Bourn —3H **39**
Avenue, The. Poole —1C **68**
Avenue, The. St L —1F **17**
  (off Oak Tree Farm Caravan Pk.)
Avenue, The. W Moor —4B **8**
Avon Av. Ring —4F **11**
Avon Bldgs. Christ —6F **43**
Avon Castle Dri. Ring —3F **11**
Avon Causeway. Hurn —4H **25**
Avoncliffe Rd. Bourn —4C **60**
Avon Clo. Bourn —1D **58**
Avon Clo. Lym —2E **51**
Avon Gdns. Brans —2D **26**
Avon M. Bourn —1C **58**
Avon Pk. Ring —1F **11**
Avon Rd. Bourn —1C **58**
Avon Rd. W Moor —6C **8**
Avon Rd. E. Christ —5E **43**
Avon Rd. W. Christ —5D **42**
Avon Run Clo. Christ —2D **62**
Avon Run Rd. Christ —2D **62**
Avon Trading Pk. Christ —6E **43**
Avon View Pde. Burt —2G **43**
Avon View Rd. Burt —2G **43**
Avon Wharf. Christ —1G **61**
Award Rd. Wim —4F **15**
Axford Clo. Bourn —2E **41**
Aylesbury Rd. Bourn —3D **58**
Aysha Clo. New M —4H **47**
Azalea Clo. St I —2C **10**
Aztec Cen. Poole —5B **36**
Azura Clo. T Leg —1F **9**

Back La. Sway —1G **31**
Badbury Clo. Broad —2A **36**
Badbury View. Wim —4F **13**
Badbury View Rd. Cor M —3D **18**
Baden Clo. New M —4H **47**
Bader Rd. Poole —5C **36**
Badgers Clo. Ashy H —2B **10**
Badgers Clo. Sway —1G **31**
Badgers Copse. New M —5A **30**

Badgers Wlk. Fern —2C **16**
Badger Way. Ver —4D **4**
Bailey Clo. New M —1B **48**
Bailey Cres. Poole —6A **36**
Baiter Gdns. Poole —6A **54**
Baker Rd. Bourn —6B **22**
Bakers Farm Rd. Ver —2C **4**
Balcombe Rd. Poole —4C **56**
Baldwin Clo. Christ —1H **61**
Balena Clo. Poole —5G **35**
Balfour Clo. Christ —5F **45**
Balfour Rd. Bourn —4H **39**
Ballam Clo. Bourn —6C **34**
Ballard Clo. New M —1H **47**
Ballard Clo. Poole —6B **54**
Ballard Rd. Poole —6A **54**
Ballards Pas. Poole —5A **54**
Balmoral Av. Bourn —4E **41**
Balmoral Rd. Poole —4G **55**
Balmoral Wlk. New M —2F **47**
Balston Rd. Poole —1E **55**
Balston Ter. Poole —5H **53**
Banbury Rd. Poole —6A **36**
Bank Chambers. Poole —3A **56**
Bank Clo. Christ —1F **61**
Bankhill Dri. Lym —6F **33**
Bankside. Lym —5F **33**
Bankside Rd. Bourn —2A **40**
Banks Rd. Poole —6F **67**
Bankview. Lym —5F **33**
Banstead Rd. Broad —6G **19**
Barberry Way. Ver —4G **5**
Barbers Ga. Poole —6H **53**
Barbers Piles. Poole —6H **53**
Barbers Wharf. Poole —6H **53**
  (off Quay, The)
Barfields. Lym —1G **51**
Bargates. Christ —6E **43**
Baring Rd. Bourn —3E **61**
Barlands Clo. Burt —3G **43**
Barn Clo. Poole —6A **34**
Barnes Clo. Bourn —2F **39**
Barnes Cres. Bourn —2F **39**
Barnes Cres. Wim —5G **13**
Barnes La. Evtn —3E **49**
Barnes Rd. Bourn —2F **39**
Barnfield. Christ —5F **45**
Barn Rd. Broad —2H **35**
Barnsfield Rd. St L —5C **10**
Barns Rd. Fern —3E **17**
Barons Rd. Bourn —5H **21**
Barrack Rd. Christ —5B **42**
Barrack Rd. W Parl —2A **24**
Barrie Rd. Bourn —2H **39**
Barrington Ct. Bourn —6F **39**
Barrow Dri. Bourn —3F **41**
Barrowgate Rd. Bourn —2C **40**
Barrowgate Way. Bourn —2D **40**
Barrow Rd. Bourn —3F **41**
Barrows La. Sway —4F **31**
Barrow View. Fern —3H **15**
Barrow Way. Bourn —3F **41**
Barrs Av. New M —1G **47**
Barrs Wood Dri. New M —1H **47**
Barrs Wood Rd. New M —1H **47**
Barry Gdns. Broad —6F **19**
Barters La. Broad —2F **35**
Bartlett Dri. Bourn —5H **41**
Barton Comn. La. New M —5H **47**
Barton Comn. Rd. New M —6H **47**
Barton Ct. Av. New M —6F **47**
Barton Ct. Rd. New M —4G **47**
Barton Croft. New M —6G **47**
Barton Dri. New M —5F **47**
Barton Grn. New M —6H **47**
Barton La. New M —5D **46**
Bartonside Rd. New M —5C **46**
Barton Way. New M —5F **47**
Barton Wood Rd. New M —6E **47**
Bascott Clo. Bourn —4C **38**
Bascott Rd. Bourn —4B **38**
Bashley Comn. Rd. New M —4G **29**
Bashley Cross Rd. New M —6D **28**
Bashley Dri. New M —5H **29**
Bashley Rd. New M —4G **29**

Bassett Rd. Poole —1F **55**
Batchelor Cres. Bourn —2B **38**
Batchelor Rd. Bourn —2B **38**
Batcombe Clo. Bourn —2A **38**
Bath Hill Ct. Bourn —4A **58**
Bath Rd. Bourn —5H **57**
Bath Rd. Lym —2H **51**
Batten Clo. Christ —6H **43**
Baverstock Rd. Poole —5D **38**
Bay Clo. Poole —1B **52**
Bay Clo. T Leg —2A **8**
Bay Hog La. Poole —5H **53**
Bays Ct. Lym —1E **51**
Bays Rd. Lym —1E **51**
Baytree Way. Christ —4F **45**
Bay View. New M —6C **46**
Beach Av. New M —6F **47**
Beach Rd. Brnk P —1C **68**
Beach Rd. Uptn —1A **52**
Beacon Clo. Evtn —4H **49**
Beacon Dri. Christ —6H **45**
Beacon Gdns. Broad —2E **35**
Beacon Pk. Cres. Poole —5A **34**
Beacon Pk. Rd. Poole —6A **34**
Beacon Rd. Bourn —5G **57**
Beacon Rd. Broad —2E **35**
Beacon Rd. Poole —6B **34**
Beaconsfield Rd. Christ —6F **43**
Beaconsfield Rd. Poole —2H **55**
Beacon Way. Broad —2E **35**
Beamish Rd. Poole —5D **36**
Bear Cross Av. Bourn —5A **22**
Beatty Clo. Ring —3E **7**
Beatty Rd. Bourn —4B **40**
Beauchamps Gdns. Bourn —5G **41**
Beau Ct. New M —2G **47**
Beaucroft La. Wim —3G **13**
Beaucroft Rd. Wim —3G **13**
Beaufort Clo. Christ —6D **44**
Beaufort Dri. Wim —4E **13**
Beaufort M. Wim —5D **12**
Beaufort Rd. Bourn —2A **60**
Beaufoys Av. Fern —2A **16**
  (in two parts)
Beaufoys Clo. Fern —2A **16**
Beaufoys Ct. Fern —3A **16**
Beaulieu Av. Christ —6C **42**
Beaulieu Clo. New M —2E **47**
Beaulieu Gdns. Caravan Pk. Christ
  —6C **42**
Beaulieu Rd. Bourn —6D **56**
Beaulieu Rd. Christ —6C **42**
Beaumont Rd. Poole —2A **68**
Beaver Ind. Est. Christ —1C **62**
Beccles Clo. Poole —5F **53**
Becher Rd. Poole —3A **56**
Beckhampton Rd. Poole —4E **53**
Beckley Copse. Christ —3A **46**
Becton La. New M —4H **47**
Becton Mead. New M —4H **47**
Bedale Way. Poole —2D **54**
Bedford Cres. Bourn —6A **42**
Bedford Rd. N. Poole —3G **37**
Bedford Rd. S. Poole —3G **37**
Beech Av. Bourn —3A **60**
Beech Av. Christ —5B **42**
Beechbank Av. Poole —4E **35**
Beech Clo. Broad —1E **35**
Beech Clo. Evtn —5H **49**
Beech Clo. Ver —4C **4**
Beech Ct. Wim —5G **13**
Beechcroft La. Ring —3D **6**
Beechcroft M. Ring —3D **6**
  (off Beechcroft La.)
Beeches, The. Bourn —5G **41**
Beechey Rd. Bourn —2A **58**
Beech La. St L —5A **10**
Beechwood Av. Bourn —3F **59**
Beechwood Av. New M —1E **47**
Beechwood Clo. Broad —2G **35**
Beechwood Gdns. Bourn —3G **59**
Beechwood Rd. W Moor —6D **8**
Belben Clo. Poole —3H **37**
Belben Rd. Poole —3G **37**
Belfield Rd. Bourn —3E **61**

Belgrave Rd. Poole —5C **56**
Belle View Mans. Bourn —4C **60**
Belle Vue Clo. Bourn —3B **60**
Belle Vue Cres. Bourn —3D **60**
Belle Vue Gdns. Bourn —3D **60**
Belle Vue Rd. Bourn —3B **60**
Belle Vue Rd. Poole —4G **55**
Belle Vue Wlk. W Parl —1G **23**
Bellflower Clo. Christ —5D **44**
Belmont Av. Bourn —3C **40**
Belmont Clo. Ver —4E **5**
Belmont Rd. New M —1A **48**
Belmont Rd. Poole —2G **55**
Belmore La. Lym —2F **51**
Belmore Rd. Lym —2F **51**
Belvedere Rd. Bourn —1A **58**
Belvedere Rd. Christ —6E **43**
Bemister Rd. Bourn —5A **40**
Benbow Cres. Poole —3A **38**
Benbridge Av. Bourn —6B **22**
Bendigo Rd. Christ —5C **42**
Benellen Av. Bourn —3E **57**
Benellen Gdns. Bourn —3E **57**
Benellen Rd. Bourn —2E **57**
Benellen Towers. Bourn —3E **57**
Bengal Rd. Bourn —4G **39**
Benmoor Rd. Poole —5G **35**
Benmore Clo. New M —3A **48**
Benmore Rd. Bourn —4A **40**
Bennett Rd. Bourn —1B **58**
Bennetts All. Poole —6H **53**
(off Quay, The)
Bennion Rd. Bourn —2E **39**
Benridge Clo. Broad —2G **35**
Benson Clo. Brans —2D **26**
Benson Rd. Poole —6B **36**
Bentley Rd. Bourn —2H **39**
Bere Clo. Poole —3B **36**
Beresford Gdns. Poole —1H **55**
Beresford Rd. Bourn —3H **59**
Beresford Rd. Lym —1E **51**
Beresford Rd. Poole —1H **55**
Berkeley Av. Poole —5G **37**
Berkeley Rd. Ver —2C **4**
Berkeley Rd. Bourn —6G **39**
Berkley Av. W Parl —6B **16**
Bernards Rd. Christ —5C **42**
Berrans Av. Bourn —5C **22**
Berryfield Rd. Hord —3E **49**
Bertram Rd. New M —1A **48**
Berwick Rd. Bourn —1G **57**
Bessborough Rd. Poole —2A **68**
Bessemer Clo. Ver —5G **5**
Beswick Av. Bourn —4F **39**
Bethia Clo. Bourn —1D **58**
Bethia Rd. Bourn —6D **40**
Betsy Clo. Brans —2D **26**
Betsy La. Brans —2D **26**
Bettiscombe Clo. Poole —3C **36**
Beverley Gdns. Bourn —2F **39**
Bexington Clo. Bourn —2A **38**
Bickerley Gdns. Ring —5B **6**
Bickerley Rd. Ring —4B **6**
Bickerley Ter. Ring —4B **6**
Bicton Rd. Bourn —2D **38**
Billington Pl. Lym —3F **51**
Bindon Clo. Poole —6A **38**
Bingham Av. Poole —2G **67**
Bingham Clo. Christ —6A **44**
Bingham Clo. Ver —5F **5**
Bingham Dri. Lym —2G **51**
Bingham Dri. Ver —5E **5**
Bingham Rd. Bourn —5A **40**
Bingham Rd. Christ —6A **44**
Bingham Rd. Ver —5E **5**
Binnie Rd. Poole —2A **56**
Birch Av. Burt —2G **43**
Birch Av. New M —6E **29**
Birch Av. W Parl —1H **23**
Birch Clo. Cor M —5D **18**
Birch Clo. Poole —4A **56**
Birch Clo. St L —4H **9**
Birchdale Rd. Wim —4F **13**

Birch Dri. Bourn —3G **41**
Birch Gro. W Moor —5B **8**
Birch Rd. St I —3D **10**
Birch Wlk. Fern —6D 16
(off Lone Pine Caravan Pk.)
Birchwood Clo. Christ —5G **45**
Birchwood M. Poole —4H **55**
Birchwood Rd. Park —4H **55**
Birchwood Rd. Poole —1B **52**
Birchy Hill. Sway —2G **31**
Birds Hill Rd. Poole —3C **54**
Birkdale Ct. Broad —6G **19**
Birkdale Rd. Broad —6G **19**
Bishop Clo. Poole —6E **39**
Bishop Ct. Ring —4C **6**
Bishop Rd. Bourn —5A **40**
Bishops Clo. Bourn —6F **41**
Bitterne Way. Lym —3F **51**
Bitterne Way. Ver —4E **5**
Blackberry La. Christ —1B **62**
Blackbird Clo. Poole —5E **35**
Blackbird Way. Brans —3E **27**
Blackburn Rd. Poole —4F **55**
Blackbush Rd. Mil S —1B **64**
Blackfield La. W Moor —4C **8**
Blackfield La. W Moor —4C **8**
Blackfield Rd. Bourn —2D **40**
Black Hill. Ver —3E **5**
Black Moor Rd. Ver —4G **5**
Blacksmith Clo. Cor M —6D **18**
Blackthorn Clo. Lym —3D **50**
Blackthorn Way. New M —1B **48**
Blackthorn Way. Ver —4F **5**
Blackwater. Christ —1A **42**
Blackwater Dri. Wim —4B **20**
Blair Av. Poole —3G **55**
Blair Clo. New M —2E **47**
Blake Dene Rd. Poole —6F **55**
Blake Hill Av. Poole —6H **55**
Blake Hill Cres. Poole —6G **55**
Blandford Clo. Poole —5F **53**
Blandford Ct. Mil S —2D **64**
Blandford Rd. Cor M —2B **18**
Blandford Rd. Uptn & Poole
—2D **52**
Blandford Rd. Wim —2A **12**
Blandford Rd. N. Poole —3A **34**
Blaney Way. Cor M —5C **18**
Blenheim Cres. Hord —1D **48**
Blenheim Dri. Christ —6D **44**
Blind La. Wim —3D **12**
Bloomfield Av. Bourn —3H **39**
Bloomfield Pl. Bourn —3H **39**
Bloxworth Rd. Poole —5B **38**
Bluebell Clo. Christ —5D **44**
Bluebell La. Poole —4F **35**
Bluff, The. Bourn —1H **39**
Blyth Clo. Christ —1B **42**
Blythe Rd. Cor M —5D **18**
Blythswood Ct. New M —6F **47**
Bob Hann Clo. Poole —2H **55**
Bockhampton Rd. Bock —6A **26**
Bodley Rd. Poole —2B **68**
Bodorgan Rd. Bourn —3H **57**
Bodowen Rd. Burt —3H **43**
Bodowen Rd. Burt —3H **43**
Bognor Rd. Broad —1F **35**
Boldre Clo. New M —5D **46**
Boldre Clo. Poole —6A **38**
Boldre La. Bold —4F **33**
Boleyn Cres. Bourn —1C **40**
Bolton Clo. Bourn —4C **60**
Bolton Cres. Fern —3E **17**
Bolton Rd. Bourn —4C **60**
Boltons, The. Mil S —3D **64**
Bond Av. W Moor —3B **8**
Bond Clo. Sway —1F **31**
Bond Rd. Poole —2D **54**
Bonham Rd. Bourn —6H **39**
Bonington Clo. Christ —6A **44**
Border Dri. Poole —2C **52**
Border Rd. Poole —2C **52**
Boreham Rd. Bourn —2D **40**
Borley Rd. Poole —5G **35**
Borthwick Rd. Bourn —2E **59**

Boscombe Cliff Rd. Bourn —4E **59**
Boscombe Gro. Rd. Bourn —2D **58**
Boscombe Overcliff Dri. Bourn
—4F **59**
Boscombe Promenade. Bosc
—4E **59**
Boscombe Spa Rd. Bourn —3D **58**
Bosley Clo. Christ —3C **42**
Bosley Way. Christ —3C **42**
Bosworth M. Bourn —1B **40**
Boulnois Av. Poole —4A **56**
Boundary Dri. Wim —3F **13**
Boundary La. St L —6G **9**
Boundary Rd. Bourn —5F **39**
Boundway. Sway —2C **30**
Bounty's La. Poole —2A **56**
Bourne Av. Bourn —4G **57**
Bourne Clo. Bourn —4F **57**
Bourne Ct. Wim —4F **13**
Bournemouth Central Bus. Pk. Bourn
—3C **58**
Bournemouth Ho. Bourn —4B **58**
Bournemouth International Airport.
Hurn —3E **25**
Bournemouth Rd. Poole —3F **55**
Bourne Valley Rd. Poole —3C **56**
Bournewood Dri. Bourn —3E **57**
Bourton Gdns. Bourn —5H **41**
Bouverie Clo. New M —4F **47**
Boveridge Gdns. Bourn —1B **40**
Bovington Clo. Poole —4D **36**
Bowden Rd. Poole —3G **37**
Bower Rd. Bourn —5D **40**
Bowland Rise. New M —3A **48**
Bowling Grn. All. Poole —5A 54
(off New Orchard)
Box Clo. Poole —6H **35**
Boyd Rd. Poole —1B **56**
Brabazon Dri. Christ —6D **44**
Brabazon Rd. Wim —2D **20**
Brabourne Av. Fern —5A **16**
Bracken Clo. Ashy H —3H **9**
Brackendale Rd. Bourn —5C **40**
Bracken Glen. Poole —2C **54**
Brackenhill. Poole —6C **56**
Brackenhill Rd. Wim —2A **14**
Bracken Rd. Bourn —3A **60**
Bracken Rd. Fern —2H **15**
Brackens Way. Poole —1B **68**
Bracken Way. Christ —4B **46**
Bracklesham Pl. New M —6F **47**
Brackley Clo. Hurn —3G **25**
Bradburne Rd. Bourn —4G **57**
Bradford Rd. Bourn —1C **40**
Bradpole Rd. Bourn —3E **41**
Bradstock Clo. Poole —5B **38**
Braemar Av. Bourn —3E **61**
Braemar Clo. Bourn —3E **61**
Braemar Dri. Christ —4G **45**
Braeside Rd. St L —3A **10**
Braeside Rd. W Moor —4D **8**
Braidley Rd. Bourn —4G **57**
Brailswood Rd. Poole —3B **54**
Braishfield Gdns. Bourn —3D **40**
Bramble La. Christ —4B **46**
Bramble Wlk. Lym —6E **33**
Bramble Way. Brans —2D **26**
Bramley Clo. Lym —3G **51**
Bramley Rd. Bourn —6E **23**
Bramley Rd. Fern —3A **16**
Brampton Rd. Poole —1B **54**
Bramshaw. New M —6C **46**
Bramshaw Gdns. Bourn —2D **40**
Bramshaw Way. New M —5D **46**
Branders Clo. Bourn —3E **61**
Branders La. Bourn —2E **61**
Branksea Av. Poole —6D **52**
Branksea Clo. Poole —6E **53**
Branksome Clo. New M —3H **47**
Branksome Ct. Poole —1C **68**
Branksome Dene Rd. Bourn —5D **56**
Branksome Hill Rd. Bourn —2D **56**
Branksome Towers. Poole —1D **68**
Branksome Wood Gdns. Bourn
—3F **57**

Branksome Wood Rd. Bourn
—2D **56**
Bransgore Gdns. Brans —2D **26**
Branwell Clo. Christ —4E **43**
Branwood Clo. Evtn —4A **50**
Brassey Clo. Bourn —4A **40**
Brassey Rd. Bourn —4H **39**
Breach La. Ring —3G **7**
Breamore Clo. New M —2E **47**
Brecon Clo. Bourn —5G **23**
Brecon Clo. New M —3A **48**
Bredy Rd. Poole —4B **36**
Bremble Clo. Poole —3G **37**
Brendon Clo. Bourn —3E **41**
Briar Clo. Christ —1B **62**
Briar Clo. Poole —2C **54**
Briarswood Rd. Poole —6C **34**
Briar Way. Wim —4B **14**
Brickenswood. New M —6C **46**
Brickfield La. Wal —6H **33**
Brickyard La. Cor M —3A **18**
Brickyard La. Fern —3G **15**
Bridge App. Poole —6H **53**
Bridge Pl. Bourn —4F **23**
Bridge Rd. Lym —1H **51**
Bridges, The. Ring —4A **6**
Bridge St. Christ —1G **61**
Bridgewater Rd. Poole —1H **55**
Bridle Clo. Uptn —6D **34**
Bridle Cres. Bourn —5A **42**
Bridle Way. Wim —3B **14**
Bridleways. Ver —3C **4**
Bridport Rd. Poole —5B **38**
Bridport Rd. Ver —3D **4**
Brierley Av. W Parl —2G **23**
Brierley Clo. Bourn —6G **23**
Brierley Rd. Bourn —1F **39**
Brightlands Av. Bourn —3D **60**
Brighton Rd. Sway —1E **31**
Bright Rd. Poole —1C **54**
Brinsons Clo. Burt —2G **43**
Brisbane Rd. Christ —4C **42**
Britannia Rd. Poole —4E **55**
Britannia Way. Christ —6D **44**
Brixey Clo. Poole —6G **37**
Brixey Rd. Poole —6G **37**
Broad Av. Bourn —4D **40**
Broadfields Clo. Mil S —2D **64**
Broadhurst Av. Bourn —1G **39**
Broadlands Av. Bourn —3D **60**
Broadlands Clo. Bourn —2D **40**
Broadlands Clo. Christ —3B **44**
Broad La. Lym —2H **51**
Broadly Clo. Lym —3D **50**
Broadmayne Rd. Poole —6B **38**
Broadmead Clo. Lym —3H **51**
Broad Mead Rd. T Leg —1B **8**
Broadmoor Rd. Cor M —5B **18**
Broadshard Ct. Ring —2C **6**
Broadshard La. Ring —2C **6**
Broads, The. Wim —3B **12**
Broadstone Way. Broad & Poole
—3F **35**
Broadwater Av. Poole —5F **55**
Broadway. S'brne —3D **60**
Broadway Gdns. Wim —5E **13**
Broadway La. Bourn —2C **40**
Broadway, The. Broad —1G **35**
Broadway, The. N'brne —5F **23**
Brockenhurst Rd. Bourn —3B **40**
Brockhills La. New M —6A **30**
Brockley Rd. Bourn —1G **39**
Brocks Pine. St L —4B **10**
Brog St. Cor M —2C **18**
Bronte Av. Christ —4E **43**
Brook Av. New M —1G **47**
Brook Av. N. New M —6H **29**
Brook Clo. Bourn —1E **39**
Brookdale Clo. Broad —1G **35**
Brook Dri. Ver —5F **5**
Brookland Clo. Penn —2E **51**
Brook La. Brans —4D **26**
Brook La. Cor M —5C **18**
Brooklyn Ct. New M —2F **47**
Brook Pk. Ind. Est. Wim —6G **13**

Brook Rd. Bourn —1E **39**
Brook Rd. Lym —3H **51**
Brook Rd. Poole —2G **55**
Brook Rd. Wim —5G **13**
Brooks Clo. Ring —5D **6**
Brookside Clo. Brans —2C **26**
Brookside Rd. Brans —2C **26**
Brookside Rd. Wim —5H **13**
Brookside Way. Christ —3G **45**
Brook Way. Christ —6E **45**
Broomfield. Fern —3C **16**
Broomfield La. Lym —1G **51**
Broomhill Clo. Lym —3D **50**
Broom Rd. Poole —4F **37**
Broughton Av. Bourn —1G **39**
Broughton Clo. Bourn —2G **39**
Brownen Rd. Bourn —5B **40**
Brownhill Rd. New M —1E **29**
Browning Av. Bourn —3F **59**
Browning Rd. Poole —1H **55**
Brownings Clo. Lym —1C **50**
Brownsea Av. Cor M —5D **18**
Brownsea Clo. New M —2E **47**
Brownsea Ct. Poole —1F **67**
Brownsea Rd. Poole —6F **67**
Brownsea View Av. Poole —6F **55**
Brownsea View Clo. Poole —6G **55**
Brudenell Av. Poole —2H **67**
Brudenell Rd. Poole —2H **67**
Brunel Clo. Ver —5G **5**
Brune Way. W Parl —6B **16**
Brunstead Pl. Poole —3D **56**
Brunstead Rd. Poole —3C **56**
Brunswick Pl. Lym —1G **51**
Bryanstone Rd. Bourn —6G **39**
Bryant Rd. Poole —5C **38**
Bryony Clo. Broad —3E **35**
Bub La. Christ —1A **62**
Buccaneers Clo. Christ —1H **61**
Buccleuch Rd. Poole —6C **56**
Buce Hayes Clo. Christ —5A **46**
Buchanan Av. Bourn —1E **59**
Buckingham Ct. Poole —4B **54**
Buckingham Rd. Bourn —6H **37**
Buckingham Wlk. New M —2E **47**
Buckland Dene. Lym —6F **33**
Buckland Gro. Christ —3G **45**
Buckland Rd. Poole —2G **55**
Buckland Ter. Poole —2G **55**
Buckland View. Lym —6F **33**
Bucklers Ct. Lym —2F **51**
Bucklers M. Lym —2F **51**
Bucklers, The. Mil S —2A **64**
Bucklers Way. Bourn —2D **40**
Buckstone Clo. Evtn —4A **50**
Buckthorn Clo. Poole —4F **35**
Bugdens La. Ver —3D **4**
  (in two parts)
Bullfinch Clo. Poole —4F **35**
Bull La. Poole —6H **53**
Bunting Rd. Fern —1H **15**
Burbridge Clo. Poole —5C **36**
Burcombe La. Hang —2G **7**
Burcombe Rd. Bourn —6E **23**
Burdock Clo. Christ —4D **44**
Bure Clo. Christ —1D **62**
Bure Haven Dri. Christ —1C **62**
Bure Homage Gdns. Christ —1D **62**
Bure Homage La. Christ —1C **62**
Bure La. Christ —2D **62**
Bure Pk. Christ —1D **62**
Bure Rd. Christ —1D **62**
Burford Clo. Christ —4B **42**
Burgess Clo. Bourn —1B **38**
Burleigh Rd. Bourn —1B **60**
Burley Clo. New M —5D **46**
Burley Clo. Poole —1G **55**
Burley Rd. Brans —5A **26**
Burley Rd. Poole —1G **55**
Burley Rd. Wink —1G **43**
Burlington Arc., The. Bourn —4H **57**
Burnaby Rd. Bourn —6E **57**
Burnbake Rd. Ver —4D **4**
Burnbrae Rd. W Parl —2F **23**
Burn Clo. Ver —5F **5**

Burnett Av. Christ —5C **42**
Burnett Rd. Christ —6D **42**
Burngate Rd. Poole —5E **53**
Burnham Dri. Bourn —6C **40**
Burnham Rd. Burt —3G **43**
Burnleigh Gdns. New M —1A **48**
Burnside. Christ —5F **45**
Burns Rd. Bourn —6B **42**
Burnt Ho. La. Brans —2C **26**
Burnt Ho. La. Pill —2H **33**
Burrard Gro. Lym —3H **51**
Burrows La. Ver —1D **4**
Burtley Rd. Bourn —4C **60**
Burton Clo. Ashy H —2H **9**
Burton Clo. Burt —4G **43**
Burtoncroft. Burt —2G **43**
Burton Hall Pl. Burt —2G **43**
Burton Rd. Christ —6A **44**
Burton Rd. Poole —4C **56**
Burt's Hill. Wim —3E **13**
Bury Rd. Poole —5B **56**
Bushell Rd. Poole —6A **36**
Bushey Rd. Bourn —4C **40**
Bushmead Dri. Ashy H —2A **10**
Bute Dri. Christ —5B **46**
Butlers La. Poul —2E **7**
Buttercup Dri. Christ —4D **44**
Buttery, The. Christ —6H **43**
Button's La. Poole —6A **54**
  (off Quay, The)
Byron Rd. Bourn —3F **59**
Byron Rd. New M —5E **47**
Byron Rd. Wim —3E **13**

Cabot La. Poole —5G **35**
Cabot Way. New M —2F **47**
Cadhay La. New M —2F **47**
Cadnam Way. Bourn —2D **40**
Cadogan Rd. Ring —4D **6**
Caesar's Way. Broad —1E **35**
Caird Av. New M —4A **48**
Cairns Clo. Christ —5D **42**
Caister Clo. Fern —3A **16**
Calder Rd. Poole —5D **36**
Caledonian Clo. Christ —6D **44**
Caledon Rd. Poole —4H **55**
Calluna Rd. Poole —5F **37**
Calmore Clo. Bourn —2D **40**
Calvin Rd. Bourn —5H **39**
Cambridge Gdns. Christ —3D **42**
Cambridge Rd. Bourn —4F **57**
Camden Clo. Bourn —4B **40**
Camden Hurst. Mil S —3B **64**
Camellia Clo. T Leg —1A **8**
Camellia Gdns. New M —3H **47**
Cameron Rd. Christ —6H **43**
Cammel Rd. W Parl —1F **23**
Campbell Rd. Bourn —2E **59**
Campbell Rd. Burt —2G **43**
Campion Gro. Christ —6B **44**
Campion Way. Lym —6G **33**
Canberra Rd. Christ —5C **42**
Candys Clo. Cor M —1E **19**
Candy's Farm Caravan Pk. Cor M
  —1E **19**
Candy's La. Cor M —1D **18**
Canford Av. Bourn —4B **38**
Canford Bottom. Wim —3B **14**
Canford Cliffs Av. Poole —5H **55**
Canford Cliffs Rd. Poole —6A **56**
Canford Cres. Poole —2A **68**
Canford Heath Rd. Poole —3A **36**
Canford Magna. Wim —1E **21**
Canford Rd. Bourn —4C **38**
Canford Rd. Poole —3B **54**
Canford View Dri. Wim —3B **14**
Canford Way. Poole —3F **37**
Cannon Clo. Broad —4F **35**
Cannon Hill Gdns. Wim —2B **14**
Cannon Hill Rd. Wim —2A **14**
  (in two parts)
Cannon St. Lym —1G **51**
Canons Wlk. Mil S —2D **64**
Canterbury Clo. W Moor —6D **8**

Canute Dri. Brans —2D **26**
Capesthorne. Christ —2D **62**
Capstone Pl. Bourn —1D **58**
Capstone Rd. Bourn —1B **58**
Captain's Row. Lym —1H **51**
Carbery Av. Bourn —3B **60**
Carbery Gdns. Bourn —2C **60**
Carbery La. Bourn —3A **60**
Carbery Row. Bourn —3A **60**
  (off Southbourne Rd.)
Cardigan Rd. Bourn —5H **39**
Cardigan Rd. Poole —3B **56**
Carey Rd. Bourn —3H **39**
Careys Rd. Bourn —1D **40**
Carisbrooke Ct. New M —2F **47**
Carisbrooke Cres. Poole —4D **52**
Carisbrooke Way. Christ —4G **45**
Carlton Av. New M —5D **46**
Carlton Gro. Poole —2H **55**
Carlton Rd. Bourn —3C **58**
Carlyle Rd. Bourn —1B **60**
Carnarvon Rd. Bourn —3E **59**
Caroline Av. Christ —1A **62**
Caroline Rd. Bourn —2D **38**
Carpenter Clo. Lym —6F **33**
Carrbridge Clo. Bourn —6F **39**
Carrbridge Rd. Bourn —6E **39**
Carrick Way. New M —4A **48**
Carrington Caravan Pk. Mil S
  —4F **65**
Carrington Clo. Mil S —2E **65**
Carrington La. Mil S —2E **65**
Carroll Av. Fern —4C **16**
Carroll Clo. Poole —1C **56**
Carsworth Way. Poole —3E **37**
Carters Av. Poole —3D **52**
Carters La. Poole —5A **54**
Cartref Clo. Ver —3D **4**
Cartwright Clo. Bourn —1E **39**
Carvers Ind. Est. Ring —4B **6**
Carvers La. Ring —4C **6**
Carysfort Rd. Bourn —3D **58**
Cashmoor Pl. Poole —6B **38**
Caslake Clo. New M —4F **47**
Cassel Av. Poole & Bourn —6D **56**
Castle Av. Christ —5G **45**
Castle Clo. Mil S —4E **65**
Castle Dene Cres. Bourn —5E **55**
Castle Ga. Clo. Bourn —3C **40**
Castle Hill. Poole —3F **55**
Castle La. E. Bourn —4G **41**
Castle La. W. Bourn —1A **40**
Castlemain Av. Bourn —2A **60**
Castleman Ct. W Moor —4B **8**
Castleman Rd. Ring —5C **6**
Castle Pde. Bourn —6B **42**
Castle Rd. Bourn —4H **39**
Castle St. Christ —1F **61**
Castle St. Poole —6A **54**
Castleton Av. Bourn —5F **23**
Castlewood. Ring —2F **11**
Catalina Clo. Christ —1C **62**
Catalina Dri. Poole —6B **54**
Caton Clo. Poole —5D **38**
Cattistock Rd. Bourn —3E **41**
Cavan Cres. Poole —4H **35**
Cavendish Corner Mobile Home Pk.
  Ring —3D **6**
Cavendish Pl. Bourn —2A **58**
Cavendish Rd. Bourn —2H **57**
Caversham Clo. Poole —4E **53**
Cawdor Rd. Bourn —6F **39**
Caxton Clo. Christ —6B **44**
Cecil Av. Bourn —6B **40**
Cecil Clo. Cor M —5E **19**
Cecil Hill. Bourn —6B **40**
Cecil Rd. Bourn —3E **59**
Cecil Rd. Poole —1H **55**
Cedar Av. Bourn —5F **23**
Cedar Av. Christ —5B **42**
Cedar Av. St L —4D **9**
Cedar Clo. Poole —5B **34**
Cedar Dri. Evtn —6D **50**
Cedar Dri. Wim —4A **14**
Cedar Gdns. New M —4F **47**

Cedar Pk. Wim —2F **15**
Cedar Pl. Brans —2D **26**
Cedars, The. Bourn —3E **57**
Cedar Way. Fern —1A **16**
Celandine Clo. Christ —5D **44**
Cellars Farm Rd. Bourn —4E **61**
Cemetery Av. Poole —1D **54**
Cemetery Rd. Wim —4D **12**
Centenary Clo. Sway —1G **31**
Centenary Rd. Bourn —2E **59**
Central Av. Cor M —4D **18**
Central Av. Poole —1A **56**
Central Dri. Bourn —3G **57**
Central Dri. St L —1F **17**
  (off Oak Tree Farm Caravan Pk.)
Centre La. Evtn —4A **50**
Centre Pl. Ring —4B **6**
Cerne Clo. Bourn —1B **40**
Chaddesley Glen. Poole —3H **67**
Chaddesley Pines. Poole —3A **68**
Chaddesley Wood Rd. Poole
  —4A **68**
Chaffey Clo. Ring —3E **7**
Chaffinch Clo. New M —3F **47**
Chaffinch Clo. Poole —4F **35**
Chalbury Clo. Poole —3E **37**
Chaldecott Gdns. Bourn —1E **39**
Chaldon Rd. Poole —3D **36**
Chalfont Av. Christ —2B **42**
Chalice Clo. Poole —3E **55**
Chalwyn Ind. Est. Poole —6E **37**
Champion Clo. Mil S —3F **65**
Chander Clo. Fern —5B **16**
Chandlers Clo. Bourn —5H **41**
Chandos Av. Poole —5C **38**
Channel Ct. New M —6E **47**
Chant Clo. Christ —6H **43**
Chantry Clo. Christ —4H **45**
Chantry, The. Bourn —3A **58**
Chapel Clo. Cor M —5C **18**
Chapel La. Brans —3C **26**
Chapel La. Cor M —6C **18**
Chapel La. Parl —3C **24**
Chapel La. Poole —5A **54**
Chapel La. Sway —3H **31**
Chapel La. Wim —4D **12**
Chapel Rise. Ring —5F **11**
Chapel Rd. Poole —3E **55**
Charborough Rd. Broad —2H **35**
Charing Clo. Ring —5C **6**
Charles Cres. New M —6H **29**
Charles Gdns. Bourn —3B **40**
Charles Keightley Ct. Wim —5F **13**
Charles Rd. Christ —5B **44**
Charles Rd. Poole —4B **54**
Charlotte Clo. Christ —1C **62**
Charlotte Clo. Poole —5E **39**
Charlton Clo. Bourn —1C **40**
Charlton Clo. Hord —2D **48**
Charminster Av. Bourn —4B **40**
Charminster Clo. Bourn —3B **40**
Charminster Pl. Bourn —3B **40**
Charminster Rd. Bourn —1A **58**
Charmouth Gro. Poole —3E **55**
Charnock Rd. Hord —2D **48**
Charnwood Av. Bourn —2B **40**
Charnwood Clo. W Moor —5C **8**
Charter Rd. Bourn —5H **21**
Chaseside. Bourn —5G **41**
Chase, The. Ring —2F **11**
Chase, The. Ver —3F **5**
Chatsworth Rd. Bourn —1B **58**
Chatsworth Rd. Poole —2F **55**
Chatsworth Way. New M —2E **47**
Chaucer Clo. Wim —3E **13**
Chaucer Dri. Mil S —2D **64**
Chaucer Rd. Poole —1B **68**
Cheam Rd. Broad —1F **35**
Cheddington Rd. Bourn —1A **40**
Chedington Clo. Poole —3C **36**
Chelmsford Rd. Poole —6B **34**
Cheltenham Rd. Poole —2G **55**
Chene Rd. Wim —5F **13**
Chequers Clo. Lym —2D **50**
Cherford Rd. Bourn —3D **38**

Cherita Ct. Poole —1D 54
Cheriton Av. Bourn —5A 42
Cheriton Way. Wim —3E 13
Cherrett Clo. Bourn —1B 38
Cherries Dri. Bourn —3G 39
Cherry Clo. Poole —2F 55
Cherry Gro. Fern —3A 16
Cherry Hill Gdns. Poole —1B 52
Cherry Hill Gro. Poole —1B 52
Cherry Tree Clo. Evtn —5H 49
Cherry Tree Clo. St L —4H 9
Cherry Tree Dri. New M —6E 29
Cherry Tree Wlk. Bourn —5F 57
Cheshire Dri. Bourn —3G 41
Chesildene Av. Bourn —2D 40
(in two parts)
Chesildene Dri. Bourn —2C 40
Chessel Av. Bourn —2F 59
Chesterfield Clo. Poole —1B 68
Chester Rd. Poole —5C 56
Chestnut Av. Bourn —3A 60
Chestnut Av. Christ —5B 42
Chestnut Av. New M —5G 47
Chestnut Gro. Wim —3E 15
Chestnut Way. Burt —2G 43
Chetnole Clo. Poole —4E 37
Cheviot Way. Ver —4D 4
Chewton Comn. Rd. Christ —4A 46
Chewton Farm Est. Christ —5C 46
Chewton Farm Rd. Christ —4C 46
Chewton Lodge. Christ —5B 46
Chewton Way. Christ —4B 46
Cheyne Gdns. Bourn —5E 57
Chichester Rd. Ring —2E 7
Chichester Wlk. Wim —2C 20
Chichester Way. Christ —2C 62
Chickerell Clo. Bourn —1B 40
Chideock Clo. Poole —1A 56
Chideock Ct. Poole —1A 56
Chigwell Rd. Bourn —4B 40
Chilcombe Rd. Bourn —2H 59
Chilfrome Clo. Poole —4B 36
Chiltern Clo. Bourn —2D 56
Chiltern Clo. New M —4F 47
Chiltern Dri. New M —5E 47
Chiltern Dri. Ver —3D 4
Chine Cres. Bourn —5F 57
Chine Cres. Rd. Bourn —5F 57
Chine Wlk. W Parl —1G 23
Chisels La. Brans —5D 26
Chislehurst Flats. Bourn —4E 57
Chorley Clo. Poole —1A 54
Christchurch Bay Rd. New M
—6F 47
Christchurch By-Pass. Christ
—6F 43
Christchurch Rd. Bourn —4B 58
Christchurch Rd. Christ & W Parl
—1D 22
Christchurch Rd. Down —5D 46
Christchurch Rd. Hurn —5H 25
Christchurch Rd. New M —5D 46
Christchurch Rd. Ring —4B 6
Christopher Cres. Poole —1A 54
Churchfield. Ver —3C 4
Churchfield Ct. Poole —4C 54
Churchfield Cres. Poole —3C 54
Churchfield Rd. Poole —4C 54
Church Hill. Mil S —2E 65
Church Hill. Ver —3C 4
Churchill Ct. New M —3F 47
Churchill Cres. Poole —1G 55
Churchill Gdns. Poole —2G 55
Churchill Rd. Bourn —2D 58
Churchill Rd. Poole —2G 55
Churchill Rd. Wim —6F 13
Church La. Christ —1F 61
Church La. Lym —2G 51
Church La. New M —4F 47
Church La. Pill —1H 33
Church La. Sway —2F 31
Church La. W Parl —5H 23
Church Mead. Lym —3G 51
Church M. Poole —3F 55

Churchmoor Rd. Wim —4A 14
Church Rd. Bourn —4D 60
Church Rd. Fern —3A 16
Church Rd. Poole —3E 55
Church Rd. T Leg —1A 8
Church St. Christ —1F 61
Church St. Poole —6H 53
Church St. Wim —4D 12
Cinnamon La. Poole —6H 53
Circle, The. Bourn —1A 40
Circle, The. Poole —2B 68
Citrine Rd. Poole —5G 53
Clare Lodge Clo. Brans —2C 26
Claremont Av. Bourn —3B 40
Claremont Rd. Bourn —3B 40
Clarence Pk. Rd. Bourn —1G 59
Clarence Rd. Poole —4E 55
Clarendon Clo. Broad —1G 35
Clarendon Pk. Lym —3F 51
Clarendon Rd. Bourn —5F 57
Clarendon Rd. Broad —2E 35
Clarendon Rd. Christ —6E 43
Clarks Clo. Ring —4C 6
Clausen Way. Lym —4E 51
Clayford Av. Fern —2H 15
Clayford Clo. Poole —3B 36
Claylake Dri. Ver —4E 5
Cleeves Clo. Poole —3H 37
Clematis Clo. Christ —4E 45
Cleveland Clo. New M —6D 46
Cleveland Gdns. Bourn —2C 58
Cleveland Rd. Bourn —2D 58
Cliff Cres. New M —6F 47
Cliff Dri. Christ —1E 63
Cliff Dri. Poole —2B 68
Cliffe Rd. New M —6E 47
Clifford Rd. Bourn —4A 40
Cliff Rd. Mil S —1A 64
Cliff Ter. New M —6F 47
Clifton Gdns. Fern —5A 16
Clifton Rd. Bourn —4B 60
Clifton Rd. Poole —5H 55
Clingan Rd. Bourn —1B 60
Clinton Clo. Christ —3B 46
Clinton Rd. Lym —6G 33
Cliveden Clo. Fern —2A 16
Clive Rd. Bourn —4H 39
Clive Rd. Christ —3F 45
Cloisters, The. Lym —2G 51
Cloisters, The. Ring —5E 7
Close, The. Ashy —3F 11
Close, The. Broad —2E 35
Close, The. New M —5H 47
Close, The. Ring —4B 6
Close, The. St I —3C 10
Close, The. Sway —1E 31
Clough's Rd. Ring —4D 6
Clover Clo. Christ —5D 44
Clover Ct. New M —1B 48
Clover Dri. Poole —4F 35
Clovers, The. Poole —5C 38
Clowes Av. Bourn —5F 61
Clyde Rd. Poole —3H 35
Coach Ho. Pl. Bourn —2A 58
Coast Guard Way. Christ —2B 62
Cobbs La. Poole —1C 54
Cobb's Rd. Wim —3F 13
Cobham Rd. Bourn —2A 40
Cobham Rd. Wim —3F 15
Cobham Way. Wim —2C 20
Cockerell Clo. Wim —2D 20
Cogdean Clo. Cor M —3E 19
Cogdeane Rd. Poole —3B 36
Cogdean Wlk. Cor M —3E 19
Cogdean Way. Cor M —3E 19
Colborne Av. Wim —3H 13
Colborne Clo. Lym —6G 33
Colbourne Clo. Brans —3C 26
Colbourne Clo. Poole —6B 54
Colehill Cres. Bourn —2B 40
Colehill La. Wim —2G 13
Coleman Rd. Bourn —2C 38
Colemere Gdns. Christ —4H 45
Colemore Rd. Bourn —6A 42
Coleridge Grn. Christ —5C 44

Coles Av. Poole —5E 53
Coles Gdns. Poole —5E 53
Colin Clo. Cor M —6D 18
College Rd. Bourn —3G 59
College Rd. Ring —4C 6
Collingbourne Av. Bourn —1B 60
Collingwood Rd. T Leg —1C 8
Collins La. Ring —4C 6
Collwood Clo. Poole —6A 36
Colonnade Rd. Bourn —2G 59
Colonnade Rd. W. Bourn —2G 59
Colt Clo. Wim —3B 14
Columbian Way. Bourn —3E 39
Columbia Rd. Bourn —3D 38
Columbia Trees La. Bourn —4E 39
Columbine Clo. Christ —4D 44
Colville Clo. Bourn —2G 59
Colville Rd. Bourn —2G 59
Comber Rd. Bourn —2H 39
Comet Way. Christ —6C 44
Comley Rd. Bourn —3H 39
Commercial Rd. Bourn —4G 57
Commercial Rd. Poole —3D 54
Compton Av. Poole —5H 55
Compton Beeches. St I —2C 10
Compton Cres. W Moor —6E 9
Compton Dri. Poole —5G 55
Compton Gdns. Poole —5G 55
Compton Rd. New M —3G 47
Condor Clo. T Leg —1F 9
Coneygar La. Fern —6G 15
Conference Pl. Lym —4H 51
Conifer Av. Poole —5F 55
Conifer Clo. Christ —2B 42
Conifer Clo. St L —3H 9
Conifer Clo. W Parl —2H 23
Conifer Cres. Lym —2D 50
Coniston Av. Bourn —5A 22
Coniston Clo. Ver —4C 4
Coniston Rd. Ring —5D 6
Connaught Clo. New M —4E 47
Connaught Cres. Poole —1A 56
Connaught Rd. Bourn —2H 59
Connell Rd. Poole —2A 54
Consort Clo. Poole —2G 55
Constitution Hill Gdns. Poole
—2E 55
Constitution Hill Rd. Poole —3D 54
Convent Meadows Caravan Site.
Christ —2G 61
Convent Wlk. Christ —1G 61
Conway Clo. New M —4H 47
Conways Dri. Poole —3E 55
Cook Clo. Ring —3E 7
Cook Row. Wim —5D 12
Coombe Av. Bourn —3G 39
Coombe Gdns. Bourn —3F 39
Coombe La. Sway —2H 31
Cooper Dean Dri. Bourn —4F 41
Coopers La. Ver —1D 4
Copeland Dri. Poole —5F 55
Copper Beech Gdns. Bourn —3F 39
Coppercourt Leaze. Wim —5E 13
(off Poole Rd.)
Coppice Av. Fern —2H 15
Coppice Clo. New M —1B 48
Coppice Clo. St I —3B 10
Coppice, The. Christ —1D 62
Coppice View. Bourn —2G 39
Copse Av. New M —3H 47
Copse Clo. Poole —4D 54
Copse Rd. New M —3H 47
Copse Rd. Ver —3D 4
Copse, The. Fern —1F 17
(off Oak Tree Farm Caravan Pk.)
Copse Way. Christ —5G 45
Copsewood Av. Bourn —4E 41
Copythorne Clo. Bourn —3D 40
Corbar Rd. Christ —5C 42
Corbiere Av. Bourn —4H 37
Corbin Av. Fern —3E 17
Corbin Ct. Lym —3D 50
Corbin Rd. Lym —2D 50
Corfe Halt Clo. Cor M —1E 19

Corfe Lodge Rd. Cor M & Broad
—1C 34
Corfe View Rd. Cor M —6C 18
Corfe View Rd. Poole —4F 55
Corfe Way. Broad —2E 35
Corhampton Rd. Bourn —1H 59
Cornelia Cres. Poole —1C 56
Cornflower Dri. Christ —4E 45
Cornford Way. Christ —5F 45
Cornish Gdns. Bourn —4F 39
Cornwallis Rd. Mil S —3B 64
Coronation Av. Bourn —4H 39
Coronation Clo. Ver —2D 4
Coronation Rd. Ver —2D 4
Corporation Rd. Bourn —2B 58
Corscombe Clo. Poole —3C 36
Cotes Av. Poole —2E 55
Cotlands Rd. Bourn —3B 58
Cotswold Clo. Ver —4D 4
Cottage Gdns. Poole —2G 55
Cottagers La. Hord —2E 49
Cotton Clo. Broad —6F 19
Countess Clo. Wim —3C 20
Countess Gdns. Bourn —5F 41
Court Clo. Christ —6A 44
Court Clo. Lym —3F 51
Courtenay Dri. Wim —3E 13
Courtenay Pl. Lym —2G 51
Courtenay Rd. Poole —3F 55
Courthill Rd. Poole —3G 55
Court Rd. Bourn —4B 40
Covena Rd. Bourn —1B 60
Coventry Clo. Cor M —1C 34
Coventry Cres. Poole —3G 35
Cove Rd. Bourn —3E 39
Cowdrey Gdns. Bourn —3F 41
Cowdry's Field. Wim —3D 12
Cowell Dri. Bourn —5G 41
Cowgrove Rd. Wim —4A 12
Cowley Rd. Lym —1E 51
Cowley Rd. Poole —5B 36
Cowleys Rd. Burt —3G 43
Cowper Av. New M —4G 47
Cowper Rd. Bourn —3H 39
Cowpitts La. Ring —1E 7
Cowslip Rd. Broad —4E 35
Cox Av. Bourn —1B 40
Cox Clo. Bourn —1B 40
Coxstone La. Ring —5C 6
Coy Pond Rd. Poole —2C 56
Crabbswood La. Sway —3C 30
Crab Orchard Way. T Leg —6C 4
Crabton Clo. Bourn —3F 59
Crabtree Clo. Burt —3G 43
Cracklewood. Fern —1E 17
Craigmoor Av. Bourn —3E 41
Craigmoor Clo. Bourn —4F 41
Craigmoor Way. Bourn —3E 41
Craigside Rd. St L —4H 9
Craigwood Dri. Fern —4C 16
Cranborne Cres. Poole —5A 38
Cranborne Pl. New M —2E 47
Cranborne Rd. Bourn —5G 57
Cranborne Rd. Wim —3E 13
Cranbrook M. Poole —1F 55
Cranbrook Rd. Poole —2F 55
Crane Dri. Ver —3C 4
Cranemoor Av. Christ —3G 45
Cranemoor Clo. Christ —3G 45
Cranemoor Gdns. Christ —3H 45
Cranes M. Poole —4B 54
Crane Way. T Leg —1F 9
Cranfield Av. Wim —4F 13
Cranleigh Clo. Bourn —2C 60
Cranleigh Ct. Bourn —2C 60
Cranleigh Gdns. Bourn —2C 60
Cranleigh Rd. Bourn —1B 60
Cranmer Rd. Bourn —5H 39
Crantock Gro. Bourn —3F 41
Cranwell Clo. Bourn —1A 38
Cranwell Clo. Brans —2D 26
Crawshaw Rd. Poole —5F 55
Creasey Rd. Bourn —6C 22
Creech Rd. Poole —2G 55
Creedy Path. Christ —1F 61

Creekmoor La. Poole —4F **35**
Crescent Dri. New M —6F **47**
Crescent Rd. Bourn —4G **57**
Crescent Rd. Poole —3A **56**
Crescent Rd. Ver —3E **5**
Crescent Rd. Wim —5E **13**
Crescent, The. Bourn —3E **59**
Crescent, The. Fern —1F 17
   (off Oak Tree Farm Caravan Pk.)
Crescent, The. New M —5D **46**
Crescent Wlk. W Parl —2G **23**
Cresta Gdns. W Parl —1G **23**
Crest Rd. Poole —1G **55**
Cribb Clo. Poole —6C **36**
Crichel Mt. Rd. Poole —2G **67**
Crichel Rd. Bourn —5A **40**
Cricket Clo. Christ —2B **62**
Crimea Rd. Bourn —6H **39**
Cringle Av. Bourn —3E **61**
Crispin Clo. Christ —5H **45**
Criterion Arc. Bourn —4H **57**
Crittall Clo. Sway —1G **31**
Crockford Clo. New M —6H **29**
Croft Clo. Cor M —4D **18**
Crofton Clo. Christ —4C **42**
Croft Rd. Brans —5D **26**
Croft Rd. Christ —6B **44**
Croft Rd. Poole —1F **55**
Croft Rd. Ring —2E **7**
Cromer Rd. Bourn —6D **40**
Cromer Rd. Poole —1A **54**
Cromwell Pl. Bourn —2H **59**
Cromwell Rd. Bourn —2H **59**
Cromwell Rd. Poole —2H **55**
Cromwell Rd. Wim —5F **13**
Crooked La. New M —5A **48**
Crosby Rd. Bourn —6E **57**
Crossmead Av. New M —3G **47**
Cross Way. Christ —4B **42**
Crossways. Evtn —4H **49**
Crossways. Poole —6C **34**
Crow Arch La. Ring —5D **6**
Crow La. Crow —5E **7**
Crown Clo. Poole —2G **55**
Crown Hill Ct. Poole —3C **54**
Crown Mead. Wim —5E **13**
Crown Wlk. Bourn —3E 59
   (off Royal Arc.)
Crusader Ct. Bourn —3D **56**
Crusader Rd. Bourn —1H **37**
Cruse Clo. Sway —1F **31**
Cucklington Gdns. Bourn —1B **40**
Cuckoo Hill Way. Brans —2E **27**
Cuckoo Rd. Poole —5E **37**
Cudnell Av. Bourn —5B **22**
Cul-de-Sac. New M —5C **46**
Culford Clo. Bourn —3F **41**
Cull Clo. Poole —5E **39**
Culliford Cres. Poole —3C **36**
Cull La. New M —5H **29**
   (in two parts)
Cullwood La. New M —6A **30**
Culverhayes Clo. Wim —3D **12**
Culverhayes Pl. Wim —3D **12**
Culverhayes Rd. Wim —3D **12**
Culver Rd. New M —3F **47**
Cumnor Rd. Bourn —4A **58**
Cunningham Clo. Bourn —2C **38**
Cunningham Clo. Christ —1C **62**
Cunningham Clo. Ring —2E **7**
Cunningham Cres. Bourn —2C **38**
Cunningham Pl. Bourn —2C **38**
Curlew Clo. Fern —2H **15**
Curlew Rd. Bourn —3D **40**
Curlew Rd. Christ —1C **62**
Curlews, The. Ver —4E **5**
Curlieu Rd. Poole —1B **54**
Curtis Rd. Poole —2G **55**
Curzon Pl. Lym —3F **51**
Curzon Rd. Bourn —1D **58**
Curzon Rd. Poole —4E **55**
Curzon Way. Christ —5F **45**
Cuthburga Rd. Wim —4E **13**
Cuthbury Clo. Wim —5C **12**

Cuthbury Gdns. Wim —4C **12**
Cutler Clo. New M —2A **48**
Cutler Clo. Poole —6E **39**
Cutlers Pl. Wim —4A **14**
Cynthia Clo. Poole —6F **37**
Cynthia Rd. Poole —6F **37**
Cypress Gro. Evtn —5H **49**
Cyril Rd. Bourn —1C **58**

Dacombe Clo. Uptn —6C **34**
Dacombe Dri. Poole —6C **34**
Dacres Wlk. Mil S —2D **64**
Dairy Clo. Christ —6H **43**
Dakota Clo. Christ —6D **44**
Dale Clo. Poole —1D **54**
Dale Rd. Poole —1D **54**
Dales Clo. Wim —3C **14**
Dales Dri. Wim —4B **14**
Dales La. Hurn —4E **25**
Dale Valley Rd. Poole —6C **36**
Dalewood Av. Bourn —6A **22**
Dalkeith Arc. Bourn —4H **57**
Dalkeith La. Bourn —4H **57**
Dalkeith Rd. Cor M —1D **34**
Dalkeith Rd. Poole —6C **56**
   (in two parts)
Dalling Rd. Poole —2C **56**
Dalmeny Rd. Bourn —4E **61**
Damerham Rd. Bourn —2D **40**
Danecourt Clo. Poole —3D **54**
Danecourt Rd. Poole —3D **54**
Danecrest Rd. Hord —2D **48**
Dane Dri. W Parl —6C **16**
Danehurst. Mil S —1A **64**
Danehurst New Rd. Tip —3A **30**
Dane Rd. Mil S —1A **64**
Danesbury Av. Bourn —3D **60**
Danes Clo. New M —4D **46**
Danestream Clo. Mil S —3D **64**
Danestream Ct. Mil S —3E **65**
Daneswood Rd. New M —2A **48**
Daniells Clo. Lym —2G **51**
Daniell's Wlk. Lym —3G **51**
Dansie Clo. Poole —3F **55**
Darby's Clo. Poole —1B **54**
Darby's La. Poole —6B **36**
   (in two parts)
Dark La. Hint —1A **46**
Dark La. New M —1F **47**
Darley Rd. Fern —6A **16**
Darracott Rd. Bourn —3G **59**
Darwin Av. Christ —4C **42**
Davenport Clo. Uptn —6C **34**
David's La. Ring —2E **11**
Davis Field. New M —3F **47**
Davis Rd. Poole —2A **56**
Dawkins Rd. Poole —4D **52**
Dawkins Way. New M —3G **47**
Dawn Clo. Bourn —3E **39**
Daws Av. Bourn —4C **38**
Daylesford Clo. Poole —5E **55**
Days Ct. Wim —5F **13**
Deacon Gdns. Bourn —6C **22**
Deacon Rd. Bourn —6C **22**
Dean Clo. Poole —4E **53**
Dean Pk. Cres. Bourn —3H **57**
Dean Pk. Rd. Bourn —3H **57**
Deans Ct. Mil S —2D **64**
Dean's Ct. La. Wim —5E **13**
Deanscroft Rd. Bourn —1G **39**
Deans Gro. Wim —2F **13**
Deansleigh Rd. Bourn —4H **41**
Deans Rd. Bourn —2H **59**
Deans, The. Bourn —3H **57**
Dean Swift Cres. Poole —1G **67**
Dear Hay La. Poole —5A **54**
Decies Rd. Poole —2F **55**
De Courtenai Clo. Bourn —6A **22**
Deepdene La. Bourn —6A **22**
Deer La. Lym —4F **33**
Deerleap Way. New M —5H **29**
Deer Pk. Clo. New M —1F **47**
Dee Way. Poole —6H **53**
De Haviland Clo. Wim —1D **20**

De Havilland Way. Christ —2B **62**
Delamere Gdns. Bourn —2G **39**
De La Warr Rd. Mil S —3C **64**
Delft M. Christ —1H **61**
Delhi Clo. Poole —4H **55**
Delhi Rd. Bourn —3G **39**
Delilah Rd. Poole —5D **52**
De Lisle Rd. Bourn —6H **39**
Delkeith Ct. Fern —5B **16**
Dell Clo. Broad —2E **35**
Dell, The. New M —5C **46**
Delph Rd. Wim —3B **20**
Delta Clo. Christ —6C **44**
De Maulley Rd. Poole —1A **68**
De Montfort Rd. Wim —2B **20**
De Mowbray Way. Lym —3F **51**
Denby Rd. Poole —3B **54**
Dene Clo. Ring —2E **7**
Deneside Copse. Penn —3D **50**
Deneve Av. Poole —4A **36**
Dene Wlk. W Parl —2G **23**
Denewood Copse. W Moor —4B **8**
Denewood Rd. Bourn —4D **56**
Denewood Rd. W Moor —3B **8**
Denham Clo. Poole —2C **36**
Denham Dri. Christ —4H **45**
Denholm Clo. Ring —2F **7**
Denison Rd. Poole —4A **36**
Denmark La. Poole —4B **54**
Denmark Rd. Bourn —4H **39**
Denmark Rd. Poole —4B **54**
Denmead. New M —1B **48**
Denmead Rd. Bourn —6B **42**
Dennis Rd. Cor M —6D **18**
   (in two parts)
Dennistoun Av. Christ —6B **44**
Derby Rd. Bourn —3C **58**
De Redvers Rd. Poole —5G **55**
Dereham Way. Poole —1B **56**
Derritt La. Brans —3A **26**
Derwent Clo. Bourn —3A **40**
Derwent Clo. Fern —3E **17**
Derwent Rd. New M —6H **29**
Derwentwater Rd. Wim —1B **20**
Devon Rd. Christ —5C **42**
Devon Rd. Poole —2C **54**
Deweys La. Ring —4B **6**
Dewlands Pk. Caravan Pk. Ver
   —3B **4**
Dewlands Rd. Ver —4B **4**
Dewlands Way. Ver —3C **4**
Dewlish Clo. Poole —3E **37**
Dial Clo. Brans —1F **27**
Diana Way. Cor M —4E **19**
Dibden Clo. Bourn —2D **40**
Dickens Rd. Bourn —6C **42**
Didcot Rd. Poole —6B **36**
Dilly La. New M —5G **47**
Dingle Rd. Bourn —3H **59**
Dingley Rd. Poole —1B **54**
Dinham Ct. New M —1B **48**
Dinham Rd. New M —1B **48**
Diprose Rd. Cor M —4E **19**
Disraeli Rd. Christ —1H **61**
Ditchbury. Lym —5F **33**
Dixies, The. Fern —2C **16**
Doe Copse Way. New M —1E **47**
Doe's La. Ver —3B **4**
Dogdean. Wim —2E **13**
Dogwood Rd. Broad —3E **35**
Dolbery Rd. Poole —3G **37**
Dolphin Av. Bourn —6G **23**
Dolphin Pl. New M —6G **47**
Dolphin Shopping Cen. Poole
   —5A **54**
Dominion Rd. Bourn —2A **38**
Donnelly Rd. Bourn —2D **60**
Donnington Dri. Christ —6D **44**
Donoughmore Rd. Bourn —3D **58**
Dorchester Gdns. Poole —2C **54**
Dorchester Rd. Oak —1H **51**
Dorchester Rd. Poole —6A **34**
Dornie Rd. Poole —2H **67**
Dorset Av. Fern —3B **16**
Dorset Lake Av. Poole —1F **67**

Dorset Rd. Bourn —2D **56**
Dorset Rd. Christ —5B **44**
Dorset Way. Poole —6A **36**
Douglas Av. Christ —1D **60**
Douglas Clo. Poole —6B **34**
Douglas Ct. Christ —1D **60**
Douglas Gdns. Poole —2A **56**
Douglas M. Bourn —2A **60**
Douglas Rd. Bourn —3C **60**
Douglas Rd. Poole —2A **56**
Doussie Clo. Poole —5B **34**
Dover Clo. Poole —4C **56**
Dover Rd. Poole —4C **56**
Doveshill Cres. Bourn —2F **39**
Doveshill Gdns. Bourn —2F **39**
Dowlands Clo. Bourn —1F **39**
Dowlands Rd. Bourn —1F **39**
Downey Clo. Bourn —3B **38**
Downlands Pl. Poole —5C **36**
Downton Clo. Bourn —2D **40**
Downton La. Down —1A **64**
Doyne Rd. Poole —3A **56**
Drake Clo. Christ —1B **62**
Drake Clo. New M —2F **47**
Drake Clo. Ring —2F **7**
Drake Rd. Poole —6A **54**
Drakes Rd. Fern —6D 16
   (off Lone Pine Caravan Pk.)
Draper Clo. Bourn —1C **38**
Draper Rd. Christ —6A **44**
Draycott Rd. Bourn —3F **39**
Dreswick Clo. Christ —1B **42**
Drew Clo. Poole —6E **39**
Drive, The. Poole —2H **55**
Droxford Rd. Bourn —1H **59**
Druids Clo. W Parl —1F **23**
Druitt Rd. Christ —5B **44**
Drummond Rd. Bourn —3D **58**
Drury Rd. Bourn —5D **56**
Dryden Clo. Ashy H —2A **10**
Dryden Pl. Mil S —2D **64**
Duart Ct. New M —2A **48**
Ducking Stool La. Christ —1F **61**
Duck Island La. Ring —5C **6**
Duck La. Bourn —1B **38**
Dudley Av. Hord —2D **48**
Dudley Gdns. Bourn —6F **23**
Dudley Pl. New M —4H **47**
Dudley Rd. Bourn —6F **23**
Dudmoor Farm Rd. Christ —1D **42**
Dudsbury Av. Fern —5B **16**
Dudsbury Cres. Fern —5B **16**
Dudsbury Gdns. W Parl —3G **23**
Dudsbury Rd. W Parl —2F **23**
Dugdell Clo. Fern —3D **16**
Dukes Dri. Bourn —6A **22**
Dukes Field. Christ —3B **42**
Dulsie Rd. Bourn —1E **57**
Dunbar Cres. Christ —3H **45**
Dunbar Rd. Bourn —1G **57**
Duncan Rd. New M —1B **48**
Duncliff Rd. Bourn —3E **61**
Dundas Rd. Poole —5C **36**
Dunedin Clo. Fern —6H **15**
Dunedin Dri. Fern —6H **15**
Dunedin Gdns. Fern —6H **15**
Dunedin Gro. Christ —6E **45**
Dunford Clo. New M —4E **47**
Dunford Rd. Poole —2H **55**
Dunkeld Rd. Bourn —1F **57**
Dunlin Clo. Christ —2D **62**
Dunnock Clo. Fern —1H **15**
Dunstans La. Poole —1E **55**
Dunyeats Rd. Broad —1H **35**
Durdells Av. Bourn —5C **22**
Durdells Gdns. Bourn —6C **22**
Durland Clo. New M —4G **47**
Durley Chine. Bourn —5F **57**
Durley Chine Ct. Bourn —5F **57**
Durley Chine Rd. Bourn —4F **57**
Durley Chine Rd. S. Bourn —5F **57**
Durley Gdns. Bourn —5F **57**
Durley Promenade. Bourn —6E **57**
Durley Rd. Bourn —5G **57**
Durley Rd. S. Bourn —5F **57**

Durlston Cres. Christ —1B **42**
Durlston Rd. Poole —5G **55**
Durnstown. Sway —1G **31**
Durrant Rd. Bourn —3G **57**
Durrant Rd. Poole —4G **55**
Durrant Way. Sway —1F **31**
Durrington Pl. Bourn —1H **59**
Durrington Rd. Bourn —6H **41**
Durweston Clo. Bourn —2B **40**

Eagle Rd. Poole —3C **56**
Earle Rd. Bourn —6E **57**
Earles Rd. T Leg —2A **8**
Earlham Dri. Poole —3G **55**
Earlsdon Way. Christ —4H **45**
East Av. Bourn —1E **57**
East Av. New M —6C **46**
E. Borough. Wim —3D **12**
  (in two parts)
Eastbrook Row. Wim —5E **13**
E. Cliff Promenade. Bourn —5A **58**
E. Cliff Way. Christ —6E **45**
East Clo. New M —5D **46**
Eastcott Clo. Bourn —6G **41**
East Dri. St L —1F **17**
  (off Oak Tree Farm Caravan Pk.)
Eastern Rd. Lym —1F **51**
Eastern Way. Mil S —3F **65**
Easter Rd. Bourn —3A **40**
Eastfield Ct. Ring —4E **7**
Eastfield La. Ring —4E **7**
East Hill. Lym —1G **51**
E. Howe La. Bourn —2E **39**
Eastlake Av. Poole —1F **55**
Eastlands. New M —4H **47**
East La. Evtn —4A **50**
E. Overcliff Dri. Bourn —5A **58**
East Quay. Poole —6A **54**
E. Quay Rd. Poole —6A **54**
East St. Poole —5A **54**
East St. Wim —5E **13**
E. View Rd. Ring —4D **6**
East Way. Bourn —4B **40**
East Way. Cor M —6D **18**
Eastwood Av. Bourn —3C **16**
Eastworth Rd. Ver —2C **4**
Eaton Rd. Poole —5C **56**
Ebblake Ind. Est. Ver —5H **5**
Ebenezer La. Ring —4B **6**
Ebor Clo. W Parl —1G **23**
Ebor Rd. Poole —1H **55**
Eccles Rd. Poole —5G **53**
Eden Gro. Wim —6F **13**
Edgarton Rd. Poole —2B **36**
Edgehill Rd. Bourn —5G **39**
Edgemoor Rd. W Moor —6F **9**
Edifred Rd. Bourn —1A **40**
Edmondsham Rd. Ver —1C **4**
Edmunds Clo. New M —4F **47**
Edward Rd. Bourn —2D **38**
  (in two parts)
Edward Rd. Christ —5B **44**
Edward Rd. Poole —2G **55**
Edwina Clo. Ring —2E **7**
Edwina Dri. Poole —3H **35**
Efford Way. Lym —3D **50**
Egdon Dri. Wim —3C **20**
Egerton Gdns. Bourn —1D **58**
Egerton Rd. Bourn —1D **58**
Egmont Clo. Ring —5E **11**
Egmont Dri. Ring —5F **11**
Egmont Gdns. Ring —5F **11**
Egmont Rd. Poole —3B **52**
Elderberry La. Christ —1B **62**
Eldon Av. New M —5E **47**
Eldon Clo. New M —5E **47**
Eldon Pl. Bourn —4D **56**
Eldon Rd. Bourn —4G **39**
Eleanor Dri. Bourn —6H **21**
Elfin Dri. Fern —2A **16**
Elgar Rd. Bourn —1F **39**
Elgin Rd. Bourn —4H **39**
Elgin Rd. Poole —6F **55**
  (in two parts)

Elise Clo. Bourn —5H **41**
Elizabeth Av. Christ —5D **42**
Elizabeth Cres. Hord —3E **49**
Elizabeth Gdns. Christ —6F **45**
Elizabeth Rd. Poole —4B **54**
Elizabeth Rd. Wim —4E **13**
Elkhams Clo. Evtn —4H **49**
Ellery Gro. Lym —6G **33**
Ellesfield Dri. W Parl —6B **16**
Ellingham Rd. New M —5D **46**
Elliott Rd. Bourn —2A **38**
Elm Av. Christ —4C **42**
Elm Av. Lym —4E **51**
Elm Av. New M —3G **47**
Elmers Way. Brans —2D **26**
Elmes Rd. Bourn —3G **39**
Elm Gdns. Bourn —2E **57**
Elmgate Dri. Bourn —6F **41**
Elmhurst Rd. Bourn —6C **22**
Elmhurst Rd. W Moor —6D **8**
Elmhurst Way. W Moor —6D **8**
Elmore Dri. Ashy H —1A **10**
Elms Av. Poole —6E **55**
Elms Clo. Poole —6E **55**
Elmstead Rd. Poole —1B **68**
Elmsway. Bourn —3C **60**
Elm Tree Wlk. W Parl —3G **23**
Elmwood Way. Christ —6H **45**
Elphinstone Rd. Christ —5B **46**
Eltham Clo. Bourn —5H **41**
Elvin Clo. Hord —1D **48**
Elwyn Rd. Bourn —2C **58**
Embankment Way. Ring —5D **6**
Emberly Clo. Fern —2E **17**
Emerson Clo. Poole —5A **54**
Emerson Rd. Poole —5A **54**
Emily Clo. Christ —4D **42**
Emsworth Rd. Lym —1G **51**
Encombe Clo. Poole —5B **38**
Endeavour Pk. Ring —5D **6**
Endfield Clo. Christ —4D **42**
Endfield Rd. Bourn —3A **40**
Endfield Rd. Christ —4C **42**
Enfield Av. Poole —1C **54**
Enfield Cres. Poole —1C **54**
Enfield Rd. Poole —1C **54**
Englands Way. Bourn —1H **37**
Ensbury Av. Bourn —4F **39**
Ensbury Clo. Bourn —4F **39**
Ensbury Ct. Bourn —3G **39**
Ensbury Pk. Rd. Bourn —3G **39**
Erica Dri. Wim —5D **18**
Ericksen Rd. Bourn —2D **38**
Erpingham Rd. Poole —3C **56**
Esmonde Way. Poole —5D **36**
Esplanade. Can C —2B **68**
Esplanade. Poole —4A **54**
Essex Av. Christ —4D **42**
Ethelbert Rd. Wim —5F **13**
Eton Gdns. Bourn —3E **57**
Ettrick Rd. Poole —6C **56**
Eucalyptus Av. St L —5C **10**
Euston Gro. Ring —5C **6**
Evans Clo. Ashy H —1A **10**
Evans Clo. Bourn —4B **38**
Evelyn Rd. Bourn —4H **39**
Evening Glade. Fern —5C **16**
Eventide Homes. Bourn —3E **41**
Everdene Ho. Bourn —4H **41**
Everest Rd. Christ —5A **44**
Everglades Rd. Fern —2B **16**
Evergreen Clo. T Leg —2A **8**
Evergreens. Ashy H —2A **10**
Evering Av. Poole —4G **37**
Evering Gdns. Poole —4G **37**
Everlea Clo. Evtn —4H **49**
Everon Gdns. New M —3H **47**
Evershot Rd. Bourn —3E **41**
Everton Rd. Hord —1D **48**
Evesham Clo. Bourn —5H **41**
Exbury Dri. Bourn —6B **22**
Excelsior Rd. Poole —4G **55**
Exeter Cres. Bourn —4H **57**
Exeter La. Bourn —4H **57**
Exeter Pk. Rd. Bourn —5H **57**

Exeter Rd. Bourn —4H **57**
Exton Rd. Bourn —6A **42**

Factory Rd. Poole —6C **34**
Fairfield. Christ —6F **43**
Fairfield Clo. Christ —6F **43**
Fairfield Clo. Lym —2G **51**
Fairfield Clo. Wim —4H **13**
Fairfield Rd. New M —6E **47**
Fairfield Rd. Wim —5F **13**
Fairies Dri. Fern —6D **16**
  (off Lone Pine Caravan Pk.)
Fairlea Rd. Lym —1G **51**
Fairlie. Ring —2E **7**
Fairlie Pk. Ring —2D **6**
Fairmile Ho. Christ —5D **42**
Fairmile Rd. Christ —3C **42**
Fairview Cres. Broad —6G **19**
Fairview Dri. Broad —6G **19**
Fairview Rd. Poole —4G **55**
Fairview Rd. Broad —6G **19**
Fairway Dri. Christ —1D **60**
Fairway Est. Bourn —1H **37**
Fairway Rd. Poole —1G **67**
Fairways. Fern —3D **16**
Fairway, The. New M —6H **47**
Fairwood Rd. Ver —4G **5**
Falcon Dri. Christ —2C **62**
Falconer Dri. Poole —3E **53**
Falkland Sq. Poole —5A **54**
Fallows, The. New M —6H **29**
Fancy Rd. Poole —5F **37**
Farcroft Rd. Poole —2F **55**
Farm Clo. Ring —3C **6**
Farm Dene Clo. Christ —5F **45**
Farmers Wlk. Evtn —4H **49**
Farmers Wlk. Wim —3D **12**
Farm La. Christ —2C **62**
Farm La. New M —6G **47**
Farm La. (North) New M —5G **47**
Farm Rd. W Moor —5B **8**
Farnham Rd. Poole —6C **38**
Farnleys Mead. Lym —3G **51**
Farriers Clo. Wim —3B **14**
Farwell Clo. Burt —2G **43**
Farwell Rd. Poole —3G **37**
Fawcett Rd. New M —3F **47**
Fawley Grn. Bourn —2D **40**
Fawn Gdns. New M —1F **47**
Felton Ct. Poole —2D **54**
Felton Cres. Christ —5H **45**
Felton Rd. Poole —2D **54**
Fenleigh Clo. New M —4H **47**
Fennel Gdns. Lym —6F **33**
Fenton Rd. Bourn —1A **60**
Fenwick Ct. Poole —2B **58**
Fern Barrow. Poole —5D **38**
Fern Clo. Burt —3G **43**
Ferncroft Gdns. Bourn —6F **23**
Ferncroft Rd. Bourn —6F **23**
Ferndale Rd. New M —6H **29**
Ferndown Cen. Fern —4B **16**
Ferndown Ind. Est. Wim —2G **15**
Fernglade. New M —2G **47**
Fernheath Clo. Bourn —3C **38**
Fernheath Rd. Bourn —2C **38**
Fernhill Clo. Poole —3E **37**
Fernhill Fields. New M —6G **29**
Fernhill La. New M —6G **29**
Fernhill Rd. New M —2G **47**
Fernlea Av. Fern —5B **16**
Fernlea Clo. Ashy H —3A **10**
Fernlea Clo. Fern —5B **16**
Fernlea Gdns. Fern —5B **16**
Fernside Av. Poole —3D **54**
Fernside Pk. Ind. Est. Wim —1G **15**
Fernside Rd. Bourn —5F **39**
Fernside Rd. Poole —2B **54**
Fernside Rd. W Moor —6C **8**
Fernway Clo. Wim —5B **14**
Fernwood Clo. St I —2D **10**
Ferris Av. Bourn —3C **40**
Ferris Clo. Bourn —3D **40**
Ferris Pl. Bourn —3D **40**

Ferry Rd. Bourn —4D **60**
Ferry Rd. Poole —6H **53**
Ferry Way. Poole —6F **67**
Feversham Av. Bourn —4E **41**
Field Pl. New M —5D **46**
Field Wlk. Lym —6F **33**
Fieldway. Christ —4F **45**
Field Way. Cor M —3E **19**
Fieldway. Ring —3D **6**
Filton Rd. Lym —1F **51**
Finchfield Av. Bourn —5B **22**
Fir Av. New M —3H **47**
Firbank Rd. Bourn —5B **40**
Fir Clo. W Moor —4C **8**
Firmain Rd. Poole —4H **37**
Firmount Clo. Evtn —4A **50**
Firs Glen Rd. Bourn —5F **39**
Firs Glen Rd. Ver —4D **4**
Firs Glen Rd. W Moor —5C **8**
Firshill. Christ —4G **45**
Firside Rd. Cor M —1C **34**
Firs La. Poole —1F **67**
First Marine Av. New M —6F **47**
Firs Way. Poole —6C **34**
Fir Tree Clo. St L —5H **9**
Firtree Cres. Hord —2D **48**
Fir Tree La. Christ —4F **45**
Fir Vale Rd. Bourn —4H **57**
Fishermans Av. Bourn —3H **59**
Fishermans Bank. Christ —2A **62**
Fishermans Rd. Poole —6A **54**
Fitzharris Av. Bourn —6A **40**
Fitzmaurice Rd. Christ —5C **42**
Fitzpain Clo. W Parl —1F **23**
Fitzpain Rd. W Parl —1F **23**
Fitzwilliam Clo. Bourn —6A **22**
Fitzworth Av. Poole —3C **52**
Flag Head Chine. Poole —3A **68**
Flaghead Rd. Poole —2A **68**
Flambard Av. Christ —4D **42**
Flambard Rd. Poole —5G **55**
Fleetsbridge Bus. Cen. Poole
—6H **35**
Fleetsbridge Retail Pk. Poole
—1H **53**
Fleets Est. Poole —1H **53**
Fleets La. Poole —6H **35**
Fletcher Clo. Bourn —2F **39**
Fletcher Rd. Bourn —2F **39**
Flexford La. Sway —5G **31**
Floral Farm. Wim —1E **21**
Florence Rd. Bourn —3E **59**
Florence Rd. Poole —3G **55**
Florin Mall. Bourn —3E **59**
  (off Royal Arc.)
Floriston Gdns. New M —2B **48**
Flower Ct. Wim —6F **13**
Flushards. Lym —2H **51**
Folly Farm La. Ashy —1E **11**
Fontmell Rd. Broad —3A **36**
Footners La. Burt —3G **43**
Ford Clo. Fern —2D **16**
Ford La. Fern —2E **17**
Foreland Clo. Christ —1B **42**
Foreland Rd. Poole —3B **52**
Forelle Cen., The. Ver —5G **5**
Forest Clo. Christ —4F **45**
Forest Clo. Ver —5H **5**
Forest Ct. New M —3H **47**
Forest Edge Clo. Ashy H —2H **9**
Forest Edge Dri. Ashy H —2H **9**
Forest Edge Rd. Crow —6G **7**
Forest Ga. Gdns. Lym —4F **51**
Forestlake Av. Ring —5F **7**
Forest La. High H —5G **7**
Forest Links Rd. Fern —6A **8**
Forest Pines. New M —1G **47**
Forest Rise. Christ —3F **45**
Forest Rd. Poole —6C **56**
Forest Rd. Thor H —1H **27**
Forest Rd. W Moor —4D **8**
Forestside Gdns. Ring —2E **7**
Forestside, The. Ver —4H **5**
Forest View. New M —6D **28**
Forest View Clo. Bourn —3A **40**

Forest View Dri. Wim —3G **15**
Forest View Rd. Bourn —2A **40**
Forest Way. Christ —3F **45**
Forest Way. Evtn —4H **49**
Forest Way. Wim —4G **15**
Forge La. Ver —4B **4**
Forsyth Gdns. Bourn —4E **39**
Fort Cumberland Pl. Poole —5D **52**
Fortescue Rd. Bourn —1A **58**
Fortescue Rd. Poole —6H **37**
Forward Dri. Lym —3E **51**
Fountain Way. Christ —1F **61**
Four Wells Rd. Wim —2A **14**
Fowlers La. Poole —5H **53**
Foxbury Rd. St L —6B **10**
Foxcote Gdns. New M —2F **47**
Foxcroft Dri. Wim —4B **14**
Foxes Clo. Ver —4D **4**
Fox Field. Evtn —4H **49**
Foxglove Clo. Christ —5E **45**
Foxglove Pl. New M —1B **48**
Foxhills. Ver —3F **5**
Foxholes Rd. Bourn —3D **60**
Foxholes Rd. Poole —1D **54**
Fox La. Wim —5C **14**
(in two parts)
Fox Pond La. Lym —3E **51**
Foxwood Av. Christ —2B **62**
Frampton Clo. New M —6A **30**
Frampton Pl. Ring —4B **6**
Frampton Rd. Bourn —5A **40**
Francesca Ct. Christ —6A **44**
Frances Rd. Bourn —3B **58**
Francis Av. Bourn —2G **37**
Francis Rd. Poole —2A **56**
Frankland Cres. Poole —4A **56**
Franklin Rd. Bourn —2A **40**
Franklin Rd. New M —1A **48**
Franklyn Clo. Poole —6B **34**
Frankston Rd. Bourn —3A **60**
Franks Way. Poole —6F **37**
Fraser Rd. Poole —4B **38**
Freda Rd. Christ —1D **60**
Frederica Rd. Bourn —5G **39**
Freemans Clo. Wim —4B **14**
Freemans La. Wim —4B **14**
French Rd. Poole —4H **35**
French's Farm Rd. Poole —6A **34**
Frensham Clo. Bourn —2G **39**
Freshwater Dri. Poole —4D **52**
Freshwater Rd. Christ —1E **63**
Friars Rd. Christ —1D **62**
Friars Wlk. New M —5G **47**
(in two parts)
Fritham Gdns. Bourn —2D **40**
Frobisher Av. Poole —4B **38**
Frobisher Clo. Christ —1B **62**
Frobisher Clo. Ring —2E **7**
Fromond Clo. Lym —6G **33**
Frost Rd. Bourn —1B **38**
Froud Way. Cor M —1C **34**
Fryer Clo. Bourn —6D **22**
Fryers Copse. Wim —3A **14**
Fryers Rd. T Leg —2A **8**
Frys La. Evtn —4H **49**
Fullerton Rd. Lym —1E **51**
Fulmar Rd. Christ —2C **62**
Fulwood Av. Bourn —6A **22**
Furlong M. Ring —4B **6**
Furlong Shopping Cen., The. Ring
—4B **6**
Furlong, The. Ring —4B **6**
Furnell Rd. Poole —6B **54**
Furze Bank La. Bourn —3E **39**
Furzebrook Clo. Poole —2C **36**
Furze Croft. New M —4G **47**
Furzehill. Wim —1E **13**
Furze Hill Dri. Poole —6G **55**
Furzelands Rd. T Leg —2A **8**
Furzey Rd. Poole —1B **52**
Furzy Whistlers Clo. Brans —2D **26**

Gainsborough Av. New M —6H **29**
Gainsborough Ct. Bourn —2H **59**

Gainsborough Rd. Ashy H —2B **10**
Gainsborough Rd. Bourn —6F **41**
Galloway Rd. Poole —3D **52**
Gallows Dri. W Parl —2F **23**
Galton Av. Christ —1D **60**
Garden Clo. New M —4G **47**
Garden La. St L —4A **10**
Gardens Ct. Poole —4C **54**
Gardens Cres. Poole —1F **67**
Gardens Rd. Poole —1F **67**
Garden Wlk. Fern —2C **16**
Gardner Rd. Christ —5C **42**
Gardner Rd. Ring —5D **6**
Garfield Av. Bourn —2D **58**
Garland Rd. Poole —3B **54**
Garrow Dri. Lym —6G **33**
Garsdale Clo. Bourn —5C **22**
Garth Clo. St L —3H **9**
Garth Rd. Bourn —4A **40**
Gaydon Rise. Bourn —1A **38**
Geneva Av. Bourn —2B **60**
Genoa Clo. Lym —4E **51**
George Rd. Cor M —4D **18**
George M. Cor M —4D **18**
Georges M. Cor M —4D **18**
Georgian Clo. Ring —3C **6**
Georgian Way. Bourn —1H **39**
Georgina Clo. Poole —5E **39**
Gerald Rd. Bourn —1A **58**
Germaine Clo. Christ —5H **45**
Gervis Cres. Poole —3E **55**
Gervis Pl. Bourn —4H **57**
Gervis Rd. Bourn —4A **58**
Gibson Rd. Poole —6C **36**
Giddylake. Wim —3E **13**
Gilbert Clo. Lym —3F **51**
Gilbert Rd. Bourn —1D **58**
Gillam Rd. Bourn —6F **23**
Gillett Rd. Poole —6E **39**
Gillingham Clo. Bourn —1C **40**
Gillingham Rd. Mil S —3D **64**
Gilpin Clo. Pill —2H **33**
Gilpin Hill. Sway —1F **31**
Gilpin Pl. Sway —1E **31**
Gipsy La. Ring —3D **6**
Gladdis Rd. Bourn —1B **38**
Gladelands Clo. Broad —1E **35**
Gladelands Pk. Fern —2D **16**
Gladelands Way. Broad —1E **35**
Glade, The. Ashy H —2A **10**
Gladstone Clo. Christ —1H **61**
Gladstone Rd. Bourn —2F **59**
Gladstone Rd. Poole —2G **55**
Gladstone Rd. E. Bourn —2F **59**
Gladstone Rd. W. Bourn —2E **59**
Glamis Av. Bourn —6G **23**
Gleadowe Av. Christ —1D **60**
Glebefields. Mil S —2D **64**
Glenair Av. Poole —4E **55**
Glenair Cres. Poole —4E **55**
Glenair Rd. Poole —4E **55**
Glenavon. New M —3A **48**
Glenavon Rd. Christ —4H **45**
Glen Clo. New M —5D **46**
Glencoe Rd. Bourn —6F **41**
Glencoe Rd. Poole —2H **55**
Glendale Av. Fern —3B **16**
Glendale Clo. Christ —2B **42**
Glendale Clo. Wim —4E **13**
Glendale Rd. Bourn —3E **61**
Glendales. New M —5D **46**
Glendene Pk. New M —6E **29**
Glendon Av. Bourn —5E **23**
Glen Dri. New M —5C **46**
Gleneagles. Christ —1D **60**
Gleneagles Av. Poole —5H **55**
Gleneagles Clo. Fern —3D **16**
Glenferness Av. Bourn —2E **57**
Glen Fern Rd. Bourn —4A **58**
Glengariff Rd. Poole —6G **55**
Glengarry. New M —3A **48**
Glengarry Way. Christ —1E **63**
Glenmeadows Dri. Bourn —6D **22**
Glenmoor Clo. Bourn —4F **39**

Glenmoor Rd. Bourn —5F **39**
Glenmoor Rd. W Parl —6A **16**
Glen Mt. Dri. Park —2F **55**
Glen Rd. Bourn —3E **59**
Glen Rd. Poole —2F **55**
Glenroyd Gdns. Bourn —3C **60**
Glenside. New M —6B **46**
Glen Spey. New M —3B **48**
Glen, The. Poole —1H **55**
Glenville Clo. Christ —3B **46**
Glenville Rd. Bourn —3E **39**
Glenville Rd. Christ —3B **46**
Glenwood Clo. W Moor —5C **8**
Glenwood La. W Moor —5C **8**
Glenwood Rd. Ver —4D **4**
Glenwood Rd. W Moor —5C **8**
Glenwood Way. W Moor —5C **8**
Glissons. Fern —1C **22**
Globe La. Poole —5A **54**
Gloucester Rd. Bourn —1F **59**
Gloucester Rd. Poole —2A **56**
Glynville Clo. Wim —2A **14**
Glynville Ct. Wim —2A **14**
Glynville Rd. Wim —2A **14**
Goathorn Clo. Poole —3D **52**
Godmanston Clo. Poole —4E **37**
Godshill Clo. Bourn —2D **40**
Golden Cres. Evtn —4H **49**
Goldfinch Clo. New M —3F **47**
Goldfinch Rd. Poole —5F **35**
Gold Mead Clo. Lym —3G **51**
Golf Links Rd. Broad —6H **19**
Golf Links Rd. Fern —1G **23**
Goliath Rd. Poole —5D **52**
Good Rd. Poole —6G **37**
Gooseberry La. Ring —4B **6**
Gordleton Ind. Est. Penn —6B **32**
Gordon Mt. Christ —4B **46**
Gordon Mt. Flats. Christ —5A **46**
Gordon Rd. Bourn —3D **58**
Gordon Rd. Christ —5A **46**
Gordon Rd. Lym —2E **51**
Gordon Rd. Poole —2C **56**
Gordon Rd. Wim —5G **53**
Gordon Rd. S. Poole —2C **56**
Gordon Way. Burt —4G **43**
Gore Grange. New M —3F **47**
Gore Rd. New M —3D **46**
Gore Rd. Ind. Est. New M —3E **47**
Gorey Rd. Poole —4H **37**
Gorleston Rd. Poole —2B **56**
Gorley Rd. Ring —1E **7**
Gorley Rd. Ring —3E **7**
Gorsecliff Rd. Bourn —4F **39**
Gorse Clo. New M —1B **48**
Gorse Clo. St L —3H **9**
Gorsefield Rd. New M —6H **29**
Gorse Hill Clo. Poole —2C **54**
Gorse Hill Cres. Poole —2C **54**
Gorse Hill Rd. Poole —2C **54**
Gorseland Ct. Fern —6B **16**
Gorse La. Poole —6C **34**
Gorse Rd. Cor M —6C **18**
Gort Rd. Bourn —2D **38**
Gort Rd. Poole —4G **35**
Gosling Clo. Poole —5D **36**
Gosport St. Lym —1H **51**
Gough Cres. Poole —4H **35**
Grafton Clo. Bourn —6A **40**
Grafton Clo. Christ —1H **61**
Grafton Gdns. Lym —4E **51**
Grafton Rd. Bourn —1A **58**
Grammar School La. Wim —5D **12**
Granby Rd. Bourn —1A **40**
Grand Av. Bourn —3A **60**
Grand Pde. Bourn —5E **23**
Grand Pde. Poole —6H **53**
Grange Clo. Evtn —5A **50**
Grange Ct. Bourn —4B **58**
Grange Gdns. Poole —5A **38**
Grange Rd. Bourn —4B **60**
Grange Rd. Broad —1G **35**
Grange Rd. Christ —6D **44**
Grange Rd. St L —5H **9**
Grange, The. Evtn —5A **50**

Grantham Rd. Bourn —2E **59**
Grantley Rd. Bourn —3F **59**
Grants Av. Bourn —1D **58**
Grants Clo. Bourn —1E **59**
*Granville Pl. Bourn —4H **57***
(off Verulam Pl.)
Granville Rd. Bourn —2G **59**
Granville Rd. Poole —2F **55**
Grasmere Clo. Christ —2B **42**
Grasmere Gdns. New M —6H **29**
Grasmere Rd. Bourn —3G **59**
Grasmere Rd. Poole —6F **67**
Gravel Hill. Poole & Wim —3A **36**
Gravel La. Ring —4B **6**
(in two parts)
Gray Clo. Poole —5D **36**
Graycot Clo. Bourn —6E **23**
Gray's Yd. Poole —6A **54**
Greaves Clo. Bourn —2E **39**
Grebe Clo. Christ —1C **62**
Grebe Clo. Mil S —3E **65**
Grebe Clo. Poole —5E **35**
Green Acre. New M —5G **47**
Green Acre Caravan Site. Christ
—6B **44**
Greenacre Clo. Poole —1C **52**
Greenacres Clo. Bourn —5G **23**
Green Acres Clo. Ring —2F **11**
Greenbanks Clo. Mil S —2D **64**
Green Bottom. Wim —2A **14**
Green Clo. Poole —6B **54**
Greenclose La. Wim —4F **13**
Greenfield Gdns. New M —5H **47**
Greenfield Rd. Poole —1C **54**
Greenfinch Clo. Poole —4F **35**
Greenfinch Wlk. High —5E **7**
Green Gdns. Poole —6B **54**
Greenhayes. Broad —3A **36**
Greenhays Rise. Wim —4E **13**
Greenhill Clo. Wim —3F **13**
Greenhill La. Wim —3F **13**
Greenhill Rd. Wim —3F **13**
Green La. Bourn —1E **39**
Green La. Christ —6A **28**
Green La. Fern —2C **22**
Green La. New M —5H **47**
Green La. Poole —1H **67**
Green La. Ring —4C **6**
Green La. Ring —6E **7**
Greenmead Av. Evtn —4H **49**
Green Pk. Bourn —4D **58**
Green Rd. Bourn —5A **40**
Green Rd. Poole —5A **54**
Greensleeves Av. Broad —5H **19**
Greensome Dri. Fern —3D **16**
Greenway Clo. Lym —2E **51**
Greenway Cres. Poole —6A **34**
Greenways. Christ —5H **45**
Greenways. Mil S —2C **64**
Greenways Av. Bourn —2C **40**
Greenwood Av. Fern —3B **16**
Greenwood Av. Poole —6G **55**
Greenwood Copse. St I —3C **10**
Greenwood Rd. Bourn —4G **39**
Greenwood Way. St I —3C **10**
Grenfell Rd. Bourn —2H **39**
Grenville Clo. Ring —2F **7**
Grenville Ct. Poole —5A **54**
Grenville Rd. Wim —5F **13**
Gresham Rd. Bourn —4A **40**
Greycot Clo. T Leg —2A **8**
Greystoke Av. Bourn —6B **22**
Griffin Ct. Wim —6F **13**
Griffiths Gdns. Bourn —6D **22**
Grosvenor Clo. Ashy H —2H **9**
Grosvenor Gdns. Bourn —3E **59**
Grosvenor M. Lym —6F **33**
Grosvenor Rd. Bourn —4E **57**
Grove Farm Meadow Caravan Pk.
Christ —3B **42**
Groveley Rd. Bourn —5D **56**
Groveley Rd. Christ —1A **62**
Grovely Av. Bourn —3F **59**
Grove Pastures. Lym —2G **51**
Grove Pl. Lym —2G **51**

Grove Rd. Bourn —4A **58**
Grove Rd. Lym —2H **51**
Grove Rd. New M —6F **47**
Grove Rd. Poole —1F **55**
Grove Rd. Wim —5F **13**
Grove Rd. E. Christ —5E **43**
Grove Rd. W. Christ —5D **42**
Grove, The. Bourn —2H **39**
Grove, The. Christ —5C **42**
Grove, The. Fern —5A **16**
Grove, The. Ver —4E **5**
Guernsey Rd. Poole —4H **37**
Guest Av. Poole —1B **56**
Guest Clo. Poole —1C **56**
Guest Rd. Poole —6B **34**
Guildhall Ct. Poole —5H **53**
(off New Orchard)
Guild Hill Rd. Bourn —3C **60**
Gulliver Clo. Poole —1G **67**
Gulliver Ct. Wim —4E **13**
Gundrymoor Trading Est. W Moor
—1C **8**
Gunville Cres. Bourn —2B **40**
Gurjun Clo. Poole —5A **34**
Gurney Rd. Cor M —5E **19**
Gussage Rd. Poole —5B **38**
Guy's Clo. Ring —4D **6**
Gwenlyn Rd. Poole —1C **52**
Gwynne Rd. Poole —2A **56**

Haarlem M. Christ —6H **43**
Hacking Rd. Poole —5G **53**
Hadden Rd. Bourn —5D **40**
Hadley Way. Broad —2E **35**
Hadow Rd. Bourn —2E **39**
Hadrian Clo. Fern —1F **23**
Hadrian Way. Cor M —3E **19**
Haglane Copse. Lym —3E **51**
Hahnemann Rd. Bourn —5G **57**
Haig Av. Poole —6A **56**
Haking Rd. Christ —6H **43**
Hale Av. New M —3H **47**
Hale Gdns. New M —3H **47**
Halewood Way. Christ —5D **42**
Halifax Way. Christ —6D **44**
Hall Rd. Bourn —2B **38**
Halstock Cres. Poole —3B **36**
Halter Path. Poole —4E **53**
(in two parts)
Halter Rise. Wim —3C **14**
Halton Clo. Brans —3D **26**
Hambledon Gdns. Bourn —1A **60**
Hambledon Rd. Bourn —6H **41**
Hamble Rd. Poole —6E **37**
Hamilton Clo. Bourn —2D **58**
Hamilton Clo. Christ —3B **62**
Hamilton Clo. Poole —5E **53**
Hamilton Ct. Mil S —3C **64**
Hamilton Cres. Poole —5E **53**
Hamilton Rd. Bourn —2D **58**
Hamilton Rd. Cor M —6E **19**
Hamilton Rd. Poole —5E **53**
Hamilton Way. New M —3E **47**
Ham La. Wim & Fern —5B **14**
Hampden La. Bourn —2H **59**
Hampreston Rd. Fern —1C **22**
Hampshire Clo. Christ —3D **42**
Hampshire Hatches La. Ring
—3H **11**
Hampshire Shopping Cen., The.
Bourn —3E **41**
Hampton Dri. Ring —2D **6**
Handley Ct. Ring —4B **6**
Hanham Rd. Cor M —6D **18**
Hanham Rd. Wim —4E **13**
Hankinson Rd. Bourn —5A **40**
Hannah Way. Lym —5B **32**
Hannington Pl. Bourn —2G **59**
Hannington Rd. Bourn —2G **59**
Hanover Grn. Poole —5D **36**
Hanover Ho. Poole —4B **54**
Harbeck Rd. Bourn —2C **40**
Harbour Clo. Poole —3H **67**
Harbour Cres. Christ —2A **62**

Harbour Hill Cres. Poole —2C **54**
Harbour Hill Rd. Poole —3C **54**
Harbour Prospect. Poole —1G **67**
Harbour Rd. Bourn —4E **61**
Harbour View Clo. Poole —2E **55**
Harbour View Rd. Poole —2E **55**
Harcombe Clo. Poole —2C **36**
Harcourt Rd. Bourn —2G **59**
Hardy Clo. New M —2F **47**
Hardy Clo. W Moor —6D **8**
Hardy Cres. Wim —6F **13**
Hardy Rd. Poole —3H **55**
Hardy Rd. W Moor —6D **8**
Hare La. New M & Hord —2B **48**
Hares Grn. Bourn —5G **41**
Harewood Av. Bourn —6F **41**
Harewood Cres. Bourn —6F **41**
Harewood Gdns. Bourn —6F **41**
Hare Wood Grn. Key —3G **65**
Harewood Pl. Bourn —1H **59**
Harford Clo. Lym —4D **50**
Harford Rd. Poole —5G **37**
Harkwood Dri. Poole —3E **53**
Harland Rd. Bourn —3E **61**
Harleston Vs. Wim —5F **13**
Harness Clo. Wim —3B **14**
Harraby Grn. Broad —2G **35**
Harrier Dri. Wim —1B **20**
Harriers Clo. Christ —5F **45**
Harrison Av. Bourn —1D **58**
Harrison Clo. Burt —2G **43**
Harrison Way. W Moor —4C **8**
Harris Way. New M —5A **30**
Harrow Clo. Brans —4D **26**
Harrow Rd. Brans —4C **26**
Harry Barrows Clo. Ring —5C **6**
Hart Clo. New M —1F **47**
Harting Rd. Bourn —6B **42**
Hartnell Ct. Cor M —6D **18**
Hartsbourne Dri. Bourn —5H **41**
Harts Way. Evtn —4H **49**
Harvester Way. Lym —5F **33**
Harvey Rd. Bourn —2G **59**
Harvey Rd. Christ —3C **20**
(in two parts)
Harwell Rd. Poole —6B **36**
Haskells Rd. Poole —6F **37**
Haslemere Av. Christ —5H **45**
Haslemere Pl. Christ —5A **46**
Hasler Rd. Poole —3B **36**
Haslop Rd. Wim —2A **14**
Hastings Rd. Bourn —3F **41**
Hastings Rd. Poole —3H **35**
Hatch Pond Rd. Poole —5A **36**
Hatfield Ct. New M —2E **47**
Hatfield Gdns. Bourn —5H **41**
Hathaway Rd. Bourn —3B **60**
Hatherden Av. Poole —2D **54**
Havelock Rd. Poole —2C **56**
Havelock Way. Christ —3F **45**
Haven Ct. Mil S —3C **64**
Haven Ct. Poole —6F **67**
Haven Gdns. New M —3H **47**
Haven Rd. Cor M —5C **18**
Haven Rd. Poole —3H **67**
Haverstock Rd. Bourn —3B **40**
Haviland M. Bourn —3E **59**
Haviland Rd. Bourn —2F **59**
Haviland Rd. Wim —2G **15**
Haviland Rd. E. Bourn —2F **59**
Hawkchurch Gdns. Poole —3C **36**
Hawk Clo. Wim —2A **14**
Hawker Clo. Wim —2D **20**
Hawkins Clo. Ring —2E **7**
Hawkins Rd. Poole —4B **38**
Hawkwood Rd. Bourn —3E **59**
Haworth Clo. Christ —4E **43**
Hawthorn Clo. New M —1A **48**
Hawthorn Dri. Poole —4F **35**
Hawthorn Dri. Sway —6F **31**
Hawthorn Rd. Bock —5A **44**
Hawthorn Rd. Bourn —5H **39**
Hawthorns, The. Christ —1B **62**
Haydon Rd. Poole —6D **56**

Hayes Av. Bourn —1E **59**
Hayes Clo. Wim —5A **14**
Hayes La. Wim —5B **14**
Hayeswood Rd. Wim —3A **14**
Haymoor Rd. Poole —6D **36**
Haynes Av. Poole —3B **54**
Haysoms Clo. New M —4H **47**
Hayward Cres. Ver —4C **4**
Haywards Farm Clo. Ver —4C **4**
Haywards La. Cor M —3C **18**
Hayward Way. Ver —4B **4**
Hazel Clo. Christ —4E **45**
Hazeldene. Broad —1G **35**
Hazel Dri. Fern —1A **16**
Hazell Av. Bourn —3D **38**
Hazel Rd. Lym —1C **50**
Hazelton Clo. Bourn —5G **41**
Hazelwood Av. New M —1E **47**
Hazelwood Dri. Ver —5F **5**
Hazlebury Rd. Poole —6G **35**
Hazlemere Dri. St L —4A **10**
Headlands Bus. Pk. Blash —1C **6**
Heads Farm Clo. Bourn —6G **23**
Heads La. Bourn —6G **23**
Headswell Av. Bourn —1G **39**
Headswell Cres. Bourn —1G **39**
Headswell Gdns. Bourn —1G **39**
Heanor Clo. Bourn —2D **38**
Heath Av. Poole —1B **54**
Heath Clo. Wim —2B **14**
Heathcote Rd. Bourn —3F **59**
Heatherbank Rd. Bourn —4E **57**
Heatherbrae La. Poole —1B **52**
Heather Clo. Bourn —1D **40**
Heather Clo. Christ —4A **46**
Heather Clo. Cor M —5E **19**
Heather Clo. St L —4A **10**
Heatherdown Rd. W Moor —6E **9**
Heatherdown Way. W Moor —6E **9**
Heather Dri. Fern —2B **16**
Heather Gdns. Hord —2E **49**
Heatherlands Rise. Poole —2H **55**
Heatherlea Rd. Bourn —3B **60**
Heather Rd. Bourn —2F **39**
Heather View Rd. Poole —6B **38**
Heather Way. Fern —2B **16**
Heath Farm Clo. Fern —6A **16**
Heath Farm Rd. Fern —6A **16**
Heath Farm Way. Fern —6A **16**
Heathfield Av. Poole —5C **38**
Heathfield Rd. W Moor —6D **8**
Heathfield Way. W Moor —6D **8**
Heathlands Av. W Parl —1F **23**
Heathlands Clo. Burt —2G **43**
Heathlands Clo. Ver —3E **5**
Heath Rd. Christ —4B **46**
Heath Rd. Hord —2D **48**
Heath Rd. St L —3H **9**
Heathwood Av. New M —5E **47**
Heathwood Rd. Bourn —5G **39**
Heathy Clo. New M —5F **47**
Heaton Rd. Bourn —3D **38**
Heavytree Rd. Poole —3F **55**
Heckford La. Poole —4B **54**
Heckford Rd. Cor M —6C **18**
Heckford Rd. Poole —3B **54**
Hedgerley. New M —5H **47**
Heights App. Poole —6C **34**
Heights Rd. Poole —5C **34**
Helyar Rd. Bourn —3F **41**
Henbury Clo. Cor M —5D **18**
Henbury Clo. Poole —3E **37**
Henbury Rise. Cor M —5D **18**
Henbury View Rd. Cor M —5C **18**
Hendford Gdns. Bourn —3F **39**
Hendford Rd. Bourn —3F **39**
Hengistbury Rd. Bourn —4D **60**
Hengistbury Rd. New M —5E **47**
Hengist Rd. Bourn —3D **58**
Henley Gdns. Bourn —6G **41**
Hennings Pk. Rd. Poole —2B **54**
Henville Rd. Bourn —2C **58**
Herbert Av. Poole —5G **37**
Herberton Rd. Bourn —2A **60**
Herbert Rd. Bourn —5D **56**

Herbert Rd. New M —2H **47**
Hercules Rd. Poole —4D **52**
Hermitage Rd. Poole —1E **55**
Herm Rd. Poole —4H **37**
Heron Clo. Sway —2F **31**
Heron Ct. Rd. Bourn —6A **40**
Heron Dri. Wim —2A **14**
Herstone Clo. Poole —4D **36**
Hesketh Clo. St I —2C **10**
Hestan Clo. Christ —1B **42**
Heston Way. W Moor —4B **8**
Hewitt Rd. Poole —3E **53**
Heysham Rd. Broad —2G **35**
Heytesbury Rd. Bourn —2B **60**
Hibberd Way. Bourn —4F **39**
Hibbs Clo. Poole —6C **34**
Hickes Clo. Bourn —1B **38**
Hickory Clo. Poole —5A **34**
Highbridge Rd. Poole —4G **55**
Highbury Clo. New M —2H **47**
Highcliffe Corner. Christ —5B **46**
Highcliffe Rd. Christ —5C **44**
Higher Blandford Rd. Cor M & Broad
—4E **19**
Higher Merley La. Cor M —2E **19**
Highfield. Lym —2F **51**
Highfield Av. Lym —2E **51**
Highfield Av. Ring —3C **6**
Highfield Clo. Cor M —6E **19**
Highfield Clo. Sway —1F **31**
Highfield Dri. Ring —2C **6**
Highfield Gdns. Sway —1F **31**
Highfield Rd. Bourn —3G **39**
Highfield Rd. Cor M —1E **35**
Highfield Rd. Lym —1E **51**
Highfield Rd. Ring —3C **6**
Highfield Rd. W Moor —3C **8**
High Howe Clo. Bourn —1A **38**
High Howe Gdns. Bourn —1A **38**
High Howe La. Bourn —1A **38**
Highland Av. Christ —4B **46**
Highland Rd. Poole —2F **55**
Highland Rd. Wim —3F **13**
Highlands Cres. Bourn —1E **39**
Highlands Rd. New M —5G **47**
Highland View Clo. Wim —4F **13**
High Mead. Fern —1C **22**
High Mead La. Fern —2C **22**
Highmoor Clo. Cor M —6D **18**
Highmoor Clo. Poole —4F **55**
Highmoor Rd. Bourn —4C **38**
Highmoor Rd. Cor M —6D **18**
Highmoor Rd. Poole —4G **55**
High Oaks Gdns. Bourn —1A **38**
High Pk. Rd. Broad —1E **35**
High Ridge Cres. New M —2A **48**
High St. Poole. Poole —6H **53**
(in two parts)
High St. Ashley Heath, Ashy H
—1A **10**
High St. Christchurch, Christ
—1F **61**
High St. Lymington, Lym —2G **51**
High St. M. Poole —5A **54**
High St. Milford-on-Sea, Mil S
—3E **65**
High St. N. Poole —4B **54**
High St. Ringwood, Ring —4B **6**
High St. Wimborne Minster, Wim
—4D **12**
Hightown Gdns. Ring —5D **6**
Hightown Rd. Ring —5C **6**
Hightown Trading Est. Ring —5D **6**
Hightrees Av. Bourn —4E **41**
High Trees Wlk. Fern —2B **16**
Highview Clo. Christ —2C **42**
Highview Gdns. Poole —6G **37**
High Way. Broad —2F **35**
Highwood Rd. Poole —3A **56**
Hilary Rd. Poole —4A **36**
Hilda Rd. Poole —1A **56**
Hiley Rd. Poole —1A **54**
Hillary Rd. Christ —5A **44**
Hillbourne Rd. Poole —3G **35**
Hillbrow Rd. Bourn —1H **59**

Hill Clo. Brans —3C **26**
Hillcrest Av. Fern —1A **16**
Hillcrest Clo. Bourn —2A **40**
Hillcrest Rd. Bourn —2A **40**
Hillcrest Rd. Cor M —6C **18**
Hillcrest Rd. Poole —2E **55**
Hilditch. Lym —5F **33**
Hill La. Brans —3C **26**
Hill La. Christ —3A **44**
Hillman Rd. Poole —2H **55**
Hillside Dri. Christ —1B **42**
Hillside Gdns. Cor M —1C **34**
Hillside M. Cor M —1C **34**
Hillside Rd. Cor M —1C **34**
Hillside Rd. Lym —2E **51**
Hillside Rd. Poole —4B **38**
Hillside Rd. Ver —2D **4**
Hill St. Poole —5A **54**
Hill Ter. Wim —1E **21**
Hilltop Clo. Fern —2H **15**
Hilltop Rd. Cor M —6E **19**
Hilltop Rd. Fern —2H **15**
Hillview Rd. Bourn —1F **39**
Hill View Rd. Fern —2A **16**
Hill Way. Lym —5F **33**
Hill Way. Ashy H —2B **10**
Hilton Clo. Poole —1E **55**
Hilton Rd. New M —1H **47**
Hinchliffe Clo. Poole —5F **53**
Hinchliffe Rd. Poole —5F **53**
Hinton Rd. Bourn —4H **57**
Hinton Wood Av. Christ —3G **45**
Hinton Wood La. Hint —3G **45**
Hive Gdns. Poole —3H **67**
Hives Way. Lym —5F **33**
Hobart Rd. New M —3F **47**
Hobbs Pk. St L —3B **10**
Hobbs Rd. Poole —5G **37**
Hoburne Farm Caravan Pk. Christ
—5E **45**
Hoburne Gdns. Christ —4E **45**
Hoburne La. Christ —4E **45**
Hodges Clo. Poole —6C **36**
Hogue Av. Bourn —6F **23**
Holbury Clo. Bourn —2E **41**
Holcombe Rd. Poole —1B **52**
Holdenhurst Av. Bourn —1A **60**
Holdenhurst Rd. Bourn —4B **58**
Holdenhurst Rd. Bourn —2F **41**
  (Holdenhurst)
Holes Bay Rd. Poole —1H **53**
Holes Clo. Hord —1D **48**
Hollands Wood Dri. New M
—6G **29**
Holland Way. Broad —6F **19**
Hollies Clo. Sway —2F **31**
Holloway Av. Bourn —6B **22**
Holly Clo. Poole —6A **34**
Holly Clo. St L —3H **9**
Holly Ct. Bourn —4F **57**
Holly Gdns. Burt —4H **43**
Holly Gdns. Mil S —2C **64**
Holly Gro. Ver —4C **4**
Holly Hedge La. Poole —5A **36**
Holly La. Christ —3A **44**
Holly La. New M —1A **48**
Holly La. Wim —4A **12**
Holly Lodge. Poole —3C **56**
Hollywood La. Lym —6F **33**
Holm Clo. Ring —2E **7**
Holme Rd. Christ —5B **46**
Holmfield Av. Bourn —6A **42**
Holm Hill La. Christ —4B **28**
Holmhurst Av. Christ —4G **45**
Holmsley Clo. Lym —3D **50**
Holmsley Rd. New M —1D **28**
Holmwood Garth. High —5F **7**
Holnest Rd. Poole —4B **36**
Holt Rd. Poole —1B **56**
Holt Rd. T Leg —2A **8**
Holworth Rd. Bourn —2A **38**
Holyrood Clo. Poole —5G **35**
Holywell Clo. Poole —2B **36**
Homedale Ho. Bourn —2H **57**

Homedene Ho. Poole —4B **54**
Home Farm Rd. Ver —3C **4**
Home Farm Way. Ver —3C **4**
Homelands Est. Christ —1D **60**
Homelands Ho. Fern —4B **16**
Homeoaks Ho. Bourn —2H **57**
Home Rd. Bourn —5D **22**
Homeside Rd. Bourn —3A **40**
Homeview Ho. Poole —4B **54**
Homewood Clo. New M —2A **48**
Honeybourne Cres. Bourn —3E **61**
Honeysuckle La. Poole —4F **35**
Honeysuckle Way. Christ —5D **44**
Hood Clo. Bourn —4D **38**
Hood Cres. Bourn —4D **38**
Hooke Clo. Poole —3E **37**
Hop Clo. Poole —6A **34**
Hopkins Clo. Bourn —3G **61**
Horace Rd. Bourn —3E **59**
Hordle La. Hord —5D **48**
Hornbeam Way. Wim —4G **13**
Horning Rd. Poole —2B **56**
Horsa Clo. Bourn —3C **60**
Horsa Ct. Bourn —3C **60**
Horsa Rd. Bourn —3C **60**
Horseshoe Clo. Wim —3B **14**
Horseshoe, The. Poole —5G **67**
Horsham Av. Bourn —5E **23**
Horton Clo. Bourn —2C **40**
Horton Rd. Ashy H —1G **9**
Horton Rd. T Leg —2A **8**
Horton Way. Ver —4B **4**
Hosker Rd. Bourn —2H **59**
Houlton Rd. Poole —3C **54**
Hounds Way. Wim —4B **14**
Hounslow Clo. Poole —5F **53**
Howard Clo. Christ —1B **62**
Howard Rd. Bourn —6C **40**
Howard Rd. Ver —3D **4**
  (in two parts)
Howards Mead. Lym —3D **50**
Howe Clo. Christ —2C **62**
Howe Clo. New M —2F **47**
Howe La. Ver —4C **4**
Howell Ho. Wim —2H **13**
Howeth Clo. Bourn —2F **39**
Howeth Rd. Bourn —3E **39**
Howlett Clo. Lym —1E **51**
Howton Clo. Bourn —6E **23**
Howton Rd. Bourn —6E **23**
Hoxley Rd. Bourn —1F **39**
Hoyal Rd. Poole —4D **52**
Hudson Clo. Poole —3G **37**
Hudson Clo. Ring —3E **7**
Hudson Davies Clo. Pill —2H **33**
Hughs Bus. Cen. Christ —6C **44**
Hull Cres. Bourn —1H **37**
Hull Rd. Bourn —1H **37**
Hull Way. Bourn —1A **38**
Humber Rd. Fern —3E **17**
Humphrey's Bri. Christ —6E **45**
Hundred La. P'mre —4H **33**
Hungerfield Clo. Brans —2C **26**
Hungerford Rd. Bourn —2D **40**
Hunter Clo. Christ —6C **44**
Hunter Clo. Wim —3C **14**
Hunters Clo. Ver —4G **5**
Huntfield Rd. Bourn —2B **40**
Huntingdon Dri. Wim —2C **20**
Huntingdon Gdns. Christ —3D **42**
Huntly Rd. Bourn —1F **57**
Hunt Rd. Christ —5A **44**
Hunt Rd. Poole —3C **54**
Huntvale Rd. Bourn —2B **40**
Hurdles, The. Christ —5C **42**
Hurn Clo. Ring —1F **11**
Hurn Ct. La. Hurn —5F **25**
Hurn Ho. Bourn —4B **58**
Hurn La. Ring —1F **11**
Hurn Rd. Christ —1B **42**
Hurn Rd. Ring —6E **11**
Hurn Way. Christ —4B **42**
Hursley Clo. Bourn —5A **42**
Hurstbourne Av. Christ —4G **45**
Hurst Clo. Christ —3C **46**

Hurst Ct. Mil S —3C **64**
Hurstdene Rd. Bourn —3C **40**
Hurst Hill. Poole —1G **67**
Hurst Rd. Mil S —4D **64**
Hurst Rd. Ring —2C **6**
Hyacinth Clo. Poole —4F **35**
Hyde Clo. Sway —1F **31**
Hyde Rd. Bourn —6E **23**
Hyde, The. New M —1E **47**
Hynesbury Rd. Christ —1E **63**
Hythe Rd. Poole —6E **37**

Ibbertson Clo. Bourn —3F **41**
Ibbertson Rd. Bourn —4F **41**
Ibbertson Way. Bourn —3F **41**
Ibbett Rd. Bourn —3E **39**
Ibsley Clo. Bourn —1C **58**
Iddesleigh Rd. Bourn —1H **57**
Iford Clo. Bourn —1D **60**
Iford Gdns. Bourn —6A **42**
Iford La. Bourn —6B **42**
Iley La. Mil S —2H **65**
Imber Dri. Christ —5H **45**
Imbrecourt. Poole —2A **68**
Inglegreen Clo. New M —4F **47**
Inglesham Way. Poole —3E **53**
Inglewood Av. Bourn —4F **41**
Inglewood Dri. New M —3H **47**
Ingram Wlk. Wim —5F **13**
Ingworth Rd. Poole —2C **56**
Insley Cres. Broad —6E **19**
Inveravon. Christ —2B **62**
Inverclyde Rd. Poole —3F **55**
Inverleigh Rd. Bourn —1A **60**
Inverness Rd. Poole —2A **68**
Ipswich Rd. Poole & Bourn
—3D **56**
Iris Rd. Bourn —4H **39**
Irvine Way. Christ —5A **44**
Irving Rd. Bourn —3A **60**
Isaacs Clo. Poole —6D **38**
Island View. New M —6C **46**
Island View Av. Christ —1D **62**
Island View Clo. Mil S —4E **65**
Island View Ct. New M —6F **47**
Island View Rd. New M —6D **46**
Ivamy Pl. Bourn —3B **38**
Ivor Rd. Cor M —1D **34**
Ivor Rd. Poole —6G **53**
Ivy Clo. St L —3H **9**
Ivy Ho. Bourn —4F **57**
Ivy Rd. Wim —3B **20**
Iwerne Clo. Bourn —1B **40**

Jackson Rd. Poole —1G **55**
Jacobean Clo. Christ —4B **46**
Jacqueline Rd. Poole —6G **37**
Jameson Rd. Bourn —4G **39**
James Rd. Poole —2C **56**
Jasmine Ct. Lym —1F **51**
Jaundrells Clo. New M —2A **48**
Jays Ct. Christ —5B **46**
Jealous La. Lym —1C **32**
Jefferson Av. Bourn —1D **58**
Jellicoe Clo. Poole —2D **54**
Jellicoe Dri. Christ —1B **62**
Jennings Rd. Poole —5G **55**
Jephcote Rd. Bourn —1B **38**
Jersey Clo. Poole —4H **37**
Jersey Rd. Poole —4H **37**
Jesmond Av. Christ —5H **45**
Jessica Av. Ver —2B **4**
Jessopp Clo. Bourn —1H **39**
Jessopp Rd. Wim —3B **14**
Jewell Rd. Bourn —3G **41**
J.J. Allen Shopping Cen. Bourn
  (off Hinton Rd.) —4H **57**
Johnson Rd. Wim —1G **15**
Johnstone Rd. Christ —1A **62**
Johnston Rd. Poole —6B **36**
Jolliffe Av. Poole —3B **54**
Jolliffe Rd. Poole —3B **54**
Jonathan Clo. Lym —6G **33**

Jopps Corner. Burt —1G **43**
Jordans La. Sway —1G **31**
Jowitt Dri. New M —3F **47**
Joyce Dickson Clo. Ring —5D **6**
Joys Rd. T Leg —2A **8**
Jubilee Clo. Cor M —4E **19**
Jubilee Clo. Ring —3E **7**
Jubilee Cres. Poole —2H **55**
Jubilee Gdns. Bourn —3F **39**
Jubilee Rd. Cor M —4E **19**
Jubilee Rd. Poole —2H **55**
Julia Clo. Christ —5H **45**
Julian's Rd. Wim —5C **12**
Julyan Av. Poole —5C **38**
Jumpers Av. Christ —5C **42**
Jumpers Rd. Christ —5D **42**
Junction Rd. Bourn —5H **39**
Junction Rd. Poole —3C **52**
Juniper Cen., The. Christ —5D **42**
Juniper Clo. Fern —1A **16**
Juniper Clo. Lym —3D **50**
Juniper Clo. T Leg —2A **8**
Jupiter Way. Cor M —3E **19**
  (in two parts)
Justin Gdns. Bourn —1G **39**

Kamptee Copse. New M —5H **29**
Kangaw Pl. Poole —5D **52**
Katherine Chance Clo. Burt —2G **43**
Katterns Clo. Christ —3C **42**
Keats Av. Mil S —2D **64**
Keeble Clo. Bourn —5F **23**
Keeble Cres. Bourn —5F **23**
Keeble Rd. Bourn —5F **23**
Keepers La. Wim —4F **15**
Keighley Av. Broad —3F **35**
Keith Rd. Bourn —1E **57**
Kellaway Rd. Poole —5D **36**
Kelly Clo. Poole —5D **36**
Kemp Rd. Bourn —5H **39**
Kenilworth Clo. New M —2H **47**
Kenilworth Ct. Christ —6E **43**
Kenilworth Ct. Poole —1B **68**
Kennard Ct. New M —2F **47**
Kennard Rd. New M —1F **47**
Kennart Rd. Poole —6H **35**
Kenneth Ct. Christ —6B **46**
Kennington Rd. Poole —5B **36**
Ken Rd. Bourn —3C **60**
Kensington Dri. Bourn —3F **57**
Kensington Pk. Mil S —3C **64**
Kent Rd. Poole —1A **56**
Kenyon Clo. Poole —6C **36**
Kenyon Rd. Poole —6C **36**
Keppel Clo. Ring —4D **6**
Kerley Rd. Bourn —5G **57**
Kerry Clo. Lym —2E **51**
Kestrel Clo. Fern —2H **15**
Kestrel Dri. Christ —1C **62**
Keswick Rd. Bourn —3F **59**
Keswick Rd. New M —6H **29**
Keswick Way. Ver —4C **4**
Keverstone Ct. Bourn —4D **58**
Keyes Clo. Christ —1C **62**
Keyes Clo. Poole —4B **38**
Keyhaven Rd. Mil S —3E **65**
Keysworth Av. New M —5F **47**
Keysworth Rd. Poole —3C **52**
Khyber Rd. Poole —2H **55**
Kilmarnock Rd. Bourn —4H **39**
Kilmington Way. Christ —5H **45**
Kiln Clo. Cor M —1C **34**
Kimberley Clo. Christ —5D **42**
Kimberley Rd. Bourn —1A **60**
Kimberley Rd. Poole —4F **55**
Kimber Rd. Bourn —2B **38**
Kimmeridge Av. Poole —5F **37**
King Clo. St L —3B **10**
Kingcup Clo. Broad —3E **35**
King Edward Av. Bourn —3H **39**
Kingfisher Clo. Bourn —1C **60**
Kingfisher Clo. W Moor —5D **8**
Kingfishers, The. Ver —4E **5**
Kingfisher Way. Christ —2C **62**

Kingfisher Way. Ring —1D 6
King George Av. Bourn —3H 39
King John Av. Bourn —5H 21
King John Clo. Bourn —6H 21
Kingland Cres. Poole —5A 54
Kingland Rd. Poole —5B 54
King Richard Dri. Bourn —6H 21
King's Arms La. Ring —4B 6
Kings Arms Row. Ring —4B 6
King's Av. Christ —1D 60
Kings Av. Poole —5H 55
Kingsbere Av. Bourn —3D 38
Kingsbere Rd. Poole —2C 54
Kingsbridge Rd. Poole —4G 55
Kingsbury's La. Ring —4B 6
Kings Clo. Lym —1F 51
Kings Clo. W Moor —6C 8
Kings Cres. Lym —1F 51
Kings Cres. Poole —5A 56
Kingsfield. Lym —3H 51
Kingsfield. Ring —5C 6
Kings La. Sway —4H 31
Kingsley Av. Bourn —3E 61
Kingsley Clo. Bourn —3E 61
Kingsmead Ct. Wim —4D 12
Kingsmill Rd. Poole —6C 36
Kings Pk. Central Dri. Bourn
—1E 59
Kings Pk. Dri. Bourn —1E 59
(in two parts)
Kings Pk. Rd. Bourn —1E 59
King's Rd. Bourn —6A 40
Kings Rd. Lym —1F 51
Kings Rd. New M —1A 48
King's Saltern Rd. Lym —3H 51
Kingston Pk. Lym —3F 51
Kingston Rd. Poole —3B 54
King St. Wim —5D 12
Kingsway. Fern —1H 15
Kingsway Clo. Christ —4D 42
Kingswell Clo. Bourn —3F 39
Kingswell Gdns. Bourn —3D 38
Kingswell Gro. Bourn —3D 38
Kingswell Rd. Bourn —3D 38
Kinross Rd. Bourn —1G 57
Kinsbourne Av. Bourn —3F 39
Kinson Av. Poole —6E 37
Kinson Gro. Bourn —5E 23
Kinson Pk. Rd. Bourn —5F 23
Kinson Rd. Bourn —4C 38
Kipling Rd. Bourn —2F 55
Kirby Clo. Poole —1D 54
Kirby Way. Bourn —3B 60
Kirkham Av. Burt —2G 43
Kirkway. Broad —1H 35
Kitchener Cres. Poole —4H 35
Kitchers Clo. Sway —1F 31
Kitscroft Rd. Bourn —6E 23
Kittiwake Clo. Bourn —1B 60
Kitwalls La. Mil S —2D 64
Kivernell Pl. Mil S —2C 64
Kivernell Rd. Mil S —3C 64
Kiwi Clo. Poole —4C 54
Knapp Clo. Christ —5E 43
Knapp Mill Av. Christ —5E 43
Knighton Heath Clo. Bourn —1A 38
Knighton Heath Ind. Est. Bourn
—3A 38
Knighton Heath Rd. Bourn —1A 38
Knighton La. Wim —4H 21
Knighton Pk. New M —5E 47
Knights Rd. Bourn —6H 21
Knightstone Gro. W Moor —5B 8
(off Moorlands Rd.)
Knightwood. New M —6C 46
Knightwood Clo. Christ —5F 45
Knobcrook Rd. Wim —3D 12
Knole Gdns. Bourn —3D 58
Knole Rd. Bourn —2D 58
Knoll Gdns. St I —3B 10
Knoll La. Cor M —3B 18
Knowland Dri. Mil S —2D 64
Knowles Clo. Christ —6A 44
Knowlton Gdns. Bourn —1B 40
Knowlton Rd. Poole —3D 36

Knyveton Rd. Bourn —3B 58
Kyrchil La. Wim —3H 13
Kyrchil Way. Wim —3H 13

Labrador Dri. Poole —6B 54
Laburnum Clo. Fern —3H 15
Laburnum Clo. Ver —4G 5
Laburnum Dri. Evtn —5A 50
Laburnum Ho. Bourn —1H 39
Lacey Cres. Poole —1E 55
Lacy Clo. Wim —3E 13
Lacy Dri. Wim —3E 13
Ladysmith Clo. Christ —6A 44
Lagado Rd. Poole —1G 67
Lagland Ct. Poole —6A 54
Lagland St. Poole —5A 54
Lagoon Clo. Poole —1F 67
Lagoon Rd. Poole —1F 67
Laidlaw Clo. Poole —5D 38
Lake Av. Poole —6D 52
Lake Cres. Poole —4E 53
Lake Dri. Poole —5C 52
(in two parts)
Lake Gro. Rd. New M —1F 47
Lake Rd. Bourn —5D 22
Lake Rd. Poole —6D 52
Lake Rd. Ver —5E 5
Lakeside. High —5E 7
Lakeside Pines. New M —1G 47
Lakeside Rd. Poole —6C 56
Lakeview Dri. High —5F 7
Lakewood Rd. Christ —4G 45
Lambs Clo. Poole —4A 36
Lambs Grn. La. Cor M —1F 19
Lampton Gdns. Bourn —4H 39
Lancaster Clo. Broad —6F 19
Lancaster Clo. Christ —6E 45
Lancaster Dri. Broad —6E 19
Lancaster Dri. Ver —3C 4
Lancaster Rd. Wim —1G 15
Lander Clo. Poole —6B 54
Landford Gdns. Bourn —3D 40
Landford Way. Bourn —3D 40
Landseer Rd. Bourn —4E 57
Lanes, The. New M —6G 29
Lane, The. Bourn —2C 58
Langdon Rd. Poole —3G 55
Langley Chase. Ring —2C 10
Langley Rd. Christ —4G 45
Langley Rd. Poole —3A 56
Langside Av. Poole —5C 38
Langton Clo. New M —5H 47
Langton Rd. Bourn —2F 59
Lansdowne Ct. Bourn —4C 58
Lansdowne Cres. Bourn —4A 58
Lansdowne Gdns. Bourn —3A 58
Lansdowne Rd. Bourn —2A 58
Lapwing Rd. Wim —2A 14
Lara Clo. Bourn —2D 40
Larch Clo. Hord —2D 48
Larch Clo. Poole —4E 35
Larch Clo. St I —3C 10
Larch Way. Fern —1A 16
Lark Rd. Christ —1C 62
Larks Clo. Fern —2H 15
Larksfield Av. Bourn —2C 40
Larkshill Clo. New M —1H 47
Larks Rise. Fern —2H 15
Lascelles Rd. Bourn —1H 59
Latch Farm Av. Christ —5E 43
Latimer Rd. Bourn —5H 39
Latimers Clo. Christ —4H 45
Laundry La. Mil S —3E 65
Laurel Clo. Christ —4F 45
Laurel Clo. Cor M —5D 18
Laurel Clo. Hord —1C 48
Laurel Clo. St L —3A 10
Laurel Dri. Broad —1H 35
Laurel Gdns. Broad —1A 34
Laurel La. St L —4A 10
Laurels, The. Fern —2A 16
Lavender Clo. Ver —4G 5
Lavender Rd. Hord —1C 48
Lavender Way. Broad —2D 34

Lavinia Rd. Poole —6G 37
Lawford Rise. Bourn —2A 40
Lawford Rd. Bourn —1A 40
Lawn Clo. Mil S —3E 65
Lawn Rd. Lym —2D 50
Lawn Rd. Mil S —3E 65
Lawns Clo. Wim —3C 14
Lawns Rd. Wim —3B 14
Lawns, The. Christ —5B 46
Lawn View. New M —6D 28
Lawrence Dri. Poole —6A 56
Lawrence Rd. Ring —1E 7
Lawson Rd. Poole —1F 55
Layard Dri. Wim —2B 20
Laymoor La. Wim —4D 14
Layton Ct. Poole —2H 55
Layton Rd. Poole —2H 55
Leamington Rd. Bourn —6A 40
Leap Hill Rd. Bourn —1G 59
Learoyd Rd. Poole —6B 36
Lea, The. Ver —4E 5
Lea Way. Bourn —5A 22
Lechlade Gdns. Bourn —5G 41
Ledbury Rd. Christ —2B 62
Ledgard Clo. Poole —3F 55
Leedam Rd. Bourn —1F 39
Leelands. Lym —4F 51
Lees Clo. Christ —1B 42
Leeson Dri. Fern —2H 15
Leeson Rd. Bourn —6E 41
Legg La. Wim —5F 13
Legion Clo. Poole —5E 53
Legion Rd. Poole —5E 53
Leicester Rd. Poole —3A 56
Leigham Vale Rd. Bourn —3B 60
Leigh Gdns. Wim —5F 13
Leigh La. Wim —4G 13
Leigh Pk. Lym —1E 51
Leigh Rd. New M —2G 47
Leigh Rd. Wim —5E 13
Lentham Clo. Poole —4B 36
Lentune Way. Lym —3F 51
Le Patourel Clo. Christ —6H 43
Leslie Rd. Bourn —5G 39
Leslie Rd. Poole —4E 55
Leven Av. Bourn —2F 57
Leven Clo. Bourn —3F 57
Levets La. Poole —5H 53
Lewens Clo. Wim —5E 13
Lewens La. Wim —4E 13
Lewesdon Dri. Broad —1F 35
Leybourne Av. Bourn —6E 23
(in two parts)
Leybourne Clo. Bourn —6E 23
Leydene Av. Bourn —4F 41
Leydene Clo. Bourn —4F 41
Leyland Rd. Poole —3A 38
Leyside. Christ —6B 44
Liberty Clo. T Leg —1F 9
Library Rd. Bourn —4H 39
Library Rd. Fern —4B 16
Library Rd. Poole —2A 56
Lilac Clo. Ring —3D 6
Lilliput Rd. Poole —1G 67
Lime Clo. Poole —1D 54
Lime Gro. Evtn —5H 49
Limited Rd. Bourn —4A 40
Linbrook Almshouses. Ring —1E 7
Lin Brook Dri. Ring —1E 7
Lincoln Av. Bourn —1D 58
Lincoln Av. Christ —3D 42
Lincoln Rd. Poole —6H 37
Lindbergh Rd. Wim —1G 15
Linden Clo. W Parl —2F 23
Linden Ct. Ring —3B 6
Linden Gdns. Ring —3B 6
Linden Rd. Bourn —2A 40
Linden Rd. Poole —1G 55
Linden Rd. W Parl —2F 23
Lindens, The. Burt —2H 43
Linden Way. Lym —1E 51
Lindsay Pk. Poole —3C 56
Lindsay Rd. Poole —3B 56
Lindsey Ct. Fern —6A 16
Lineside. Burt —5G 43

Linford Clo. New M —1G 47
Linford Rd. Ring —2E 7
Lingdale Rd. Bourn —1B 60
Ling Rd. Poole —5E 37
Lingwood Av. Christ —1A 62
Linhorns La. New M —6G 29
Link Mall. Poole —5A 54
(off Dolphin Shopping Cen.)
Link Rise. Cor M —5E 19
Links Dri. Christ —4B 42
Linkside Av. Bourn —5E 41
Links Rd. Poole —5H 55
Links View Av. Poole —6A 56
Linmead Dri. Bourn —5C 22
Linnet Clo. Poole —5E 7
Linnet Ct. New M —3F 47
Linnet Rd. Poole —5F 35
Linnies La. Sway —4E 31
Linthorpe Rd. Poole —3C 54
Linwood Rd. Bourn —6B 40
Lionheart Clo. Bourn —6H 21
Lions Hill Way. Ashy H —3G 9
Lions La. Ashy H —4H 9
Lions Wood. St L —3A 10
Lisle Clo. Lym —2F 51
Litchford Rd. New M —1H 47
Lit. Barrs Dri. New M —1H 47
Little Ct. Poole —1B 68
Littlecroft Av. Bourn —2B 40
Lit. Croft Rd. Poole —1F 55
Lit. Dene Copse. Lym —3D 50
Lit. Dewlands. Ver —3B 4
Littledown Av. Bourn —6E 41
Littledown Dri. Bourn —6E 41
Lit. Forest Rd. Bourn —2F 57
Lit. Lonnen. Wim —1H 13
Littlemead Clo. Bourn —6G 35
Littlemoor Av. Bourn —1H 37
Livingstone Rd. Bourn —3H 59
Livingstone Rd. Christ —6H 43
Livingstone Rd. Poole —1F 55
Livingstone Rd. Wim —5G 13
Llewellin Clo. Poole —6C 34
Llewellyn Clo. Poole —5C 34
Loch Rd. Poole —2A 56
Lockerley Clo. Lym —3G 51
Locksley Dri. Fern —6A 16
Lockyers Dri. Fern —3D 16
Lockyers Rd. Cor M —3E 19
Loders Clo. Poole —2B 36
Lodge Clo. Poole —3A 56
Lodge Rd. Christ —5C 42
Lodge Rd. Lym —2D 50
Loewy Cres. Poole —3H 37
Lombard Av. Bourn —2B 60
Lombardy Clo. Ver —4F 5
Lone Pine Caravan Pk. Fern
—6D 16
Lone Pine Dri. W Parl —6C 16
Lone Pine Way. W Parl —1H 23
Longacre Dri. Fern —5A 16
Longbarrow Clo. Bourn —4F 41
Longfield Dri. Bourn —5C 22
Longfield Dri. W Parl —3G 23
Longfield Rd. Hord —3F 49
Longfleet Dri. Poole & Wim
—5C 36
Longfleet Rd. Poole —4B 54
Long La. Ring —6D 6
Long La. Wim —2F 13
Longleat Gdns. New M —2E 47
Longmeadow La. Poole —5E 35
Long Rd. Bourn —1E 39
Longspee Rd. Wim —3B 20
Lonnen Rd. Wim —2H 13
Lonnen Wood Clo. Wim —1A 14
Lonsdale Rd. Bourn —6H 39
Loraine Av. Christ —5C 46
Lord Clo. Poole —6D 36
Lorne Pk. Rd. Bourn —4A 58
Love La. Mil S —2D 64
Lwr. Ashley Rd. New M —2B 48
Lwr. Blandford Rd. Broad —2H 35
Lwr. Buckland Rd. Lym —6F 33

Lwr. Golf Links Rd. Broad —6H **19**
Lwr. Meadend Rd. Sway —2D **30**
Lwr. Pennington La. Lym —3F **51**
Lwr. Woodside. Lym —5G **51**
Lowther Gdns. Bourn —2C **58**
Lowther Rd. Bourn —1A **58**
Lucas Rd. Poole —1G **55**
Lucerne Av. Bourn —2B **60**
Lucerne Rd. Mil S —3D **64**
Luckham Clo. Bourn —3B **40**
Luckham Gdns. Bourn —3C **40**
Luckham Pl. Bourn —3B **40**
Luckham Rd. Bourn —3B **40**
Luckham Rd. E. Bourn —3B **40**
Lucky La. Pill —2H **33**
Lulworth Av. Poole —6E **53**
Lulworth Cres. Poole —6E **53**
Lulworth Ho. Bourn —4B **58**
Lumby Dri. Ring —3D **6**
Lumby Dri. Caravan Pk. Ring
—3D **6**
Luscombe Rd. Poole —5G **55**
Luther Rd. Bourn —5H **39**
Lych Ga. Ct. Ring —5E **7**
Lydford Gdns. Bourn —3C **38**
Lydford Rd. Bourn —3C **38**
Lydgate. Mil S —2H **33**
Lydlinch Clo. W Parl —2F **23**
Lydwell Clo. Bourn —6B **22**
Lyell Rd. Poole —1G **55**
Lyme Cres. Christ —5H **45**
Lymefields. Mil S —1E **65**
Lymington Rd. Christ —6E **45**
Lymington Rd. Evtn —5S **52**
Lymington Rd. New M & Lym
—4G **47**
Lymore La. Mil S —5A **50**
Lymore Valley. Mil S —6A **50**
Lyndale Clo. Mil S —2E **65**
Lyndhurst Rd. Bock —1B **44**
Lyndhurst Rd. Christ —5C **44**
Lyne's La. Ring —4B **6**
Lynn Rd. Poole —5D **36**
Lynric Clo. New M —6G **47**
Lynton Cres. Christ —2B **42**
Lynwood Clo. Fern —2B **16**
Lynwood Dri. Wim —3C **20**
Lyon Av. New M —2H **47**
Lyon Rd. Poole —3A **38**
Lysander Clo. Christ —6E **45**
Lystra Rd. Bourn —2A **40**
Lytchett Dri. Broad —3F **35**
Lytchett Minster & Upton By-Pass.
Ly Min & Uptn —5A **34**
Lytchett Way. Poole —1B **52**
Lyteltane Rd. Lym —3F **51**
Lytham Rd. Broad —2G **35**
Lytton Rd. Bourn —2C **58**

Mabey Av. Bourn —3F **39**
Macandrew Rd. Poole —2B **68**
Macaulay Rd. Broad —1G **35**
McIntyre Rd. Hurn —3F **25**
McKinley Rd. Bourn —5E **57**
Maclaren Rd. Bourn —2H **39**
Maclean Rd. Bourn —2B **38**
McWilliam Clo. Poole —5E **39**
McWilliam Rd. Bourn —3A **40**
Madeira Rd. Bourn —4A **58**
Madeira Rd. Poole —2H **55**
Madeira Wlk. Lym —2H **51**
Madeline Clo. Poole —6F **37**
Madeline Cres. Poole —6F **37**
Madison Av. Bourn —1D **58**
Magdalen La. Christ —1E **61**
Magna Clo. Bourn —5B **22**
Magna Gdns. Bourn —5B **22**
Magna Rd. Wim & Bourn —3E **21**
Magnolia Clo. Bourn —2E **61**
Magnolia Clo. Ver —5G **5**
Magnolia Ho. Bourn —1H **39**
Magpie Clo. Bourn —2C **40**
Magpie Gro. New M —3F **47**
Mag's Barrow. W Parl —1G **23**

Maidment Clo. Bourn —1A **38**
Malan Clo. Poole —5C **36**
Malcomb Clo. Bourn —4E **61**
Mallard Clo. Bourn —4C **40**
Mallard Clo. Christ —1C **62**
Mallard Clo. Hord —2F **49**
Mallard Rd. Bourn —4D **40**
Mallard Rd. Wim —2A **14**
Mallory Clo. Christ —5B **44**
Mallow Clo. Broad —2E **35**
Mallows, The. New M —1B **48**
Malmesbury Pk. Pl. Bourn —2C **58**
Malmesbury Pk. Rd. Bourn —1A **58**
Malmesbury Rd. St L —4A **10**
Maloren Way. W Moor —6E **9**
Malthouse. Poole —5A **54**
Maltings, The. Poole —4C **54**
Malvern Clo. Bourn —2A **40**
Malvern Rd. Bourn —2A **40**
Manchester Rd. Sway —1F **31**
Mandale Clo. Bourn —1C **38**
Mandale Rd. Bourn —2B **38**
Manderley. Mil S —4E **65**
Manning Av. Christ —4E **45**
Mannings Heath Rd. Poole —3F **37**
*Mannington Pl. Bourn —4G **57***
(off Commercial Rd.)
Mannington Way. W Moor —5B **8**
Manor Av. Poole —4G **37**
Manor Clo. Fern —4C **16**
Manor Clo. Mil S —1D **64**
Manor Ct. Ring —3B **6**
Manor Farm Clo. New M —4F **47**
Manor Farm Rd. Bourn —5D **22**
Manor Gdns. Ring —3B **6**
Manor Gdns. Ver —3D **4**
Manor La. Ver —4D **4**
Manor Pk. Poole —2H **53**
Manor Rd. Bourn —4B **58**
Manor Rd. Christ —1E **61**
Manor Rd. Mil S —1D **64**
Manor Rd. New M —2G **47**
Manor Rd. Ver —3D **4**
Manor Way. Ver —2D **4**
Mansel Clo. Poole —6E **39**
Mansfield Av. Poole —3G **55**
Mansfield Clo. Poole —3G **55**
Mansfield Clo. W Parl —1F **23**
Mansfield Rd. Bourn —4G **39**
Mansfield Rd. Poole —3G **55**
Mansfield Rd. Ring —4B **6**
Manton Clo. Ham —5E **9**
Manton Rd. Poole —4E **53**
(in two parts)
Maple Clo. Christ —6H **45**
Maple Clo. New M —6H **47**
Maple Dri. Fern —1A **16**
Maple Rd. Bourn —5H **39**
Maple Rd. Poole —4B **54**
Mapperton Clo. Poole —3D **36**
Marabout Clo. Christ —6A **44**
Marchwood Rd. Bourn —2E **39**
Margards La. Ver —4B **4**
(in two parts)
Marian Clo. Cor M —1C **34**
Marianne Rd. Poole —5E **39**
Marianne Rd. Wim —2A **14**
Marian Rd. Cor M —1C **34**
Marina Clo. Bosc —4E **59**
Marina Dri. Poole —6F **55**
Marina, The. Bourn —4E **59**
Marina Towers. Bosc —4E **59**
Marina View. Christ —2D **60**
Marine Dri. New M —6E **47**
Marine Dri. E. New M —6F **47**
Marine Dri. W. New M —6D **46**
Marine Rd. Bourn —4B **60**
Mariners Ct. Lym —3H **51**
Market Clo. Poole —5A **54**
Market Pl. Ring —4B **6**
Market St. Poole —6H **53**
Market Way. Wim —5F **13**
Markham Av. Bourn —5F **23**
Markham Clo. Bourn —4F **23**

Markham Rd. Bourn —5A **40**
Mark's La. New M —5G **29**
Marks Rd. Bourn —2H **39**
Marlborough Pl. Lym —6F **33**
Marlborough Pl. Wim —4F **13**
Marlborough Rd. Bourn —4E **57**
Marlborough Rd. Poole —3G **55**
Marley Av. New M —1E **47**
Marley Clo. New M —2F **47**
Marley Mt. Sway —2C **30**
Marline Rd. Poole —1H **55**
Marlott Rd. Poole —2A **54**
Marlow Dri. Christ —2B **42**
Marlpit Dri. Christ —3A **46**
Marlpit La. New M —3G **29**
Marmion Grn. Christ —6B **44**
Marnhull Rd. Poole —3B **54**
Marpet Clo. Bourn —5B **22**
Marquis Way. Bourn —6G **21**
Marram Clo. Lym —5G **33**
Marryat Ct. Christ —6B **46**
Marryat Rd. New M —2F **47**
Marshal Rd. Poole —4H **35**
Marshfield. Wim —2H **13**
Marsh La. Christ —3D **42**
(Fairmile, in two parts)
Marsh La. Christ —1H **61**
(in two parts)
Marsh La. Lym —5F **33**
Marsh La. Poole —6A **34**
Marshwood Av. Poole —3D **36**
Marston Clo. New M —6H **29**
Marston Gro. Christ —4G **45**
Marston Rd. New M —6H **29**
Marston Rd. Poole —5H **53**
Martello Pk. Poole —2B **68**
Martello Rd. Poole —6A **56**
Martello Rd. S. Poole —1B **68**
Martells, The. New M —6H **47**
Martin Clo. Poole —6F **35**
Martindale Av. Wim —4B **14**
(in two parts)
Martingale Clo. Uptn —6D **34**
Martins Clo. Fern —2C **16**
Martins Dri. Fern —1C **16**
Martin's Hill Clo. Burt —4G **43**
Martins Hill La. Burt —4G **43**
Martins Way. Fern —2C **16**
Marwell Clo. Bourn —6F **41**
Maryland Ct. Mil S —3B **64**
Maryland Gdns. Mil S —3B **64**
Maryland Rd. Poole —3C **52**
Mary La. W Moor —5B **8**
Masters Ct. Bourn —4F **57**
Masterson Clo. Christ —6H **43**
Matcham La. Hurn —4H **25**
Matlock Rd. Fern —6A **16**
Maturin Clo. Lym —2F **51**
Maundeville Cres. Christ —5B **42**
Maundeville Rd. Christ —5C **42**
Maureen Clo. Poole —6F **37**
Maurice Rd. Bourn —5D **40**
Mavis Rd. Bourn —4B **40**
Maxwell Rd. Bourn —5A **40**
Maxwell Rd. Broad —2D **34**
Maxwell Rd. Poole —2B **68**
May Av. Lym —6F **33**
Mayfair Gdns. Bourn —1C **38**
Mayfield Av. Poole —4A **56**
Mayfield Clo. Fern —3A **16**
Mayfield Dri. Fern —3A **16**
Mayfield Pk. Cor M —3E **19**
Mayfield Rd. Bourn —3H **39**
Mayfield Way. Fern —3A **16**
Mayflower Clo. Lym —2H **51**
Mayford Rd. Poole —1D **56**
May Gdns. Bourn —2A **38**
May Gdns. Christ —3B **46**
May La. Pill —2H **33**
Maylyn Rd. Bcn H —3A **34**
Mead Clo. Broad —4G **35**
Mead End Rd. Sway —2D **30**
Meadowbank. Poole —5G **34**
Meadow Clo. Brans —3C **26**
Meadow Clo. Ring —2D **6**

Meadow Clo. W Parl —2F **23**
Meadow Ct. Bourn —2A **40**
Meadow Ct. Clo. Bourn —2A **40**
Meadow Farm La. Cor M —3D **18**
Meadow Gro. Ver —4F **5**
Meadow Land. Christ —1B **62**
Meadowlands. Lym —1D **50**
Meadow La. Burt —3G **43**
(in two parts)
Meadow Rise. Broad —6F **19**
Meadow Rd. Lym —3E **51**
Meadow Rd. New M —1H **47**
Meadow Rd. Ring —3D **6**
Meadows Caravan Site, The. New M
—4F **47**
Meadows Clo. Poole —5C **34**
Meadows Dri. Poole —6C **34**
Meadowsweet Rd. Poole —5E **35**
Meadow, The. New M —5C **46**
Meadow View Rd. Bourn —1A **58**
Meadow Way. New M —6G **47**
Meadow Way. Ring —3D **6**
Meadow Way. Ver —4E **5**
Mead Rd. Lym —3D **50**
Meadway, The. Christ —3F **45**
Medina Way. Christ —1E **63**
Medlar Clo. Burt —4H **43**
Medway Rd. Fern —3E **17**
Meeting Ho. La. Ring —4B **6**
Melbourne Rd. Bourn —1C **58**
Melbourne Rd. Christ —4C **42**
Melbury Av. Poole —6H **37**
Melbury Clo. Fern —5B **16**
Melbury Clo. Lym —2F **51**
Mellstock Rd. Poole —2A **54**
Melrose Ct. New M —2A **48**
Melverley Gdns. Wim —4F **13**
Melville Rd. Bourn —5G **39**
Mendip Clo. New M —3H **47**
Mendip Clo. Ver —4D **4**
Mendip Rd. Ver —3D **4**
Mentone Rd. Poole —4E **55**
Meon Rd. Bourn —1H **59**
Meredith Clo. Christ —6A **44**
Meriden Clo. Poole —2B **68**
Meridians, The. Christ —1D **60**
Merino Way. W Moor —6D **8**
Merlewood Clo. Bourn —3H **57**
Merley Ct. Touring Pk. Wim
—2H **19**
Merley Dri. Christ —5A **46**
Merley Gdns. Wim —2B **20**
Merley Ho. La. Wim —2H **19**
Merley La. Wim —2B **20**
Merley Pk. Rd. Ashtn —3F **19**
Merley Ways. Wim —1A **20**
Merlin Clo. High —5E **7**
Merlin Way. Christ —2C **62**
Mermaid Ct. Bosc —4E **59**
Merrifield Av. Broad —6H **19**
Merrifield Clo. Broad —5H **19**
Merrifield Dri. Broad —5H **19**
Merrifield. Wim —1G **13**
Merritown La. Hurn —4D **24**
Merrivale Av. Bourn —2C **60**
Merrow Av. Poole —6D **38**
Merryfield Clo. Brans —3C **26**
Merryfield La. Bourn —1E **39**
Merryweather Est. Ring —3E **7**
Merton Gro. Ring —3B **6**
Methuen Clo. Bourn —2C **58**
Methuen Rd. Bourn —2B **58**
Methuen Rd. Poole —3H **35**
Meyrick Clo. Brans —4C **26**
Meyrick Pk. Cres. Bourn —1H **57**
Meyrick Rd. Bourn —4B **58**
Michelgrove Rd. Poole —4E **59**
Michelmersh Grn. Bourn —3D **40**
Mickleham Clo. Poole —5D **38**
Middle Comn. Rd. Penn —2C **65**
Middlebere Cres. Poole —3C **52**
Middlehill Dri. Wim —3B **14**
Middlehill Rd. Wim —2H **13**
Middle La. Ring —4C **6**
Middle Rd. Bourn —6E **23**

Middle Rd. Lym —2F **51**
Middle Rd. Poole —1C **54**
Middle Rd. Sway —1F **31**
Middle Rd. Tip —3B **30**
Middleton Rd. Bourn —3G **39**
Middleton Rd. Ring —3C **6**
Midland Rd. Bourn —4H **39**
Midway Path. Poole —6G **67**
Midwood Av. Bourn —4F **41**
Milborne Cres. Poole —6A **38**
Milbourne Rd. Fern —3A **16**
Milburn Clo. Bourn —3E **57**
Milburn Rd. Bourn —3D **56**
Milestone Rd. Poole —1B **54**
Milford Clo. W Moor —5D **8**
Milford Ct. Mil S —2E **65**
Milford Cres. Mil S —2E **65**
Milford Dri. Bourn —6B **22**
Milford Pl. Mil S —4E **65**
Milford Rd. Evtn —5A **50**
Milford Rd. New M —4H **47**
Milford Trading Est. Mil S —3E **65**
Millar Rd. Christ —6H **43**
Millbank Ho. Wim —4E **13**
Miller Clo. New M —1A **48**
Millfield. Poole —6G **35**
Millhams Clo. Bourn —5D **22**
Millhams Dri. Bourn —5D **22**
Millhams Rd. Bourn —4C **22**
Millhams St. Christ —1F **61**
Millhams St. N. Christ —1F **61**
Mill Hill Clo. Poole —4F **55**
Mill La. Christ —5B **46**
Mill La. Hurn —5H **25**
Mill La. Lym —1H **51**
Mill La. Penn —4H **31**
Mill La. Poole —5F **55**
(in two parts)
Mill La. Wim —4D **12**
Mill Meadow. Mil S —2C **64**
Mill Rd. Christ —5E **43**
Mill Rd. N. Bourn —2D **40**
Mill Rd. S. Bourn —3D **40**
Millstream Clo. Poole —6G **35**
Millstream Clo. Wim —5E **13**
Millstream Trading Est. Ring
—6C **6**
Mill St. Cor M —1A **18**
Millyford Clo. New M —5D **46**
Milne Rd. Poole —4H **35**
Milner Rd. Bourn —5E **57**
Milton Clo. Poole —4H **55**
Milton Gro. New M —3H **47**
Milton Mead. New M —3F **47**
Milton Rd. Bourn —2A **58**
Milton Rd. Poole —4H **55**
Milton Rd. Wim —3E **13**
Milverton Clo. Christ —4G **45**
Mimosa Av. Wim —3B **20**
Minstead Rd. Bourn —2E **39**
Minster View. Wim —4E **13**
Minster Way. Poole —6B **34**
Minterne Rd. Bourn —3A **40**
Minterne Rd. Christ —1A **62**
Minterne La. Poole —2G **67**
Mission La. Broad —3G **35**
Mission Rd. Broad —3G **35**
Mitchell Clo. New M —6G **47**
Mitchell Rd. Poole —5D **36**
Mitchell Rd. Wim —2G **15**
Moat Ct. Bourn —2D **56**
Moat La. New M —4F **47**
Moffat Rd. Christ —6H **43**
Molefields. Mil S —2E **65**
Molyneaux Rd. New M —2B **48**
Moneyfly Rd. Ver —4F **5**
Monks Clo. W Moor —1E **17**
Monkshood Clo. Christ —4D **44**
Monks Way. Bourn —6G **21**
Monkswell Grn. Christ —1H **61**
Monkton Clo. Fern —2B **16**
Monkton Cres. Poole —5A **38**
Monkworthy Dri. Ashy H —2B **10**
Monmouth Dri. Ver —5F **5**
Monmouth Ct. Ring —4B **6**

Monmouth Dri. Ver —5F **5**
Monsal Av. Fern —6A **16**
Montacute Way. Wim —3C **20**
Montague Rd. Bourn —3H **59**
Montagu Pk. Christ —6A **46**
Montagu Rd. Christ —6B **46**
Monteray Dri. Hord —1D **48**
Montgomery Av. Bourn —2D **38**
Montrose Clo. Ver —3D **4**
Montrose Dri. Bourn —3D **38**
Monument La. Lym —6H **33**
Moonrakers Way. Christ —4G **45**
Moorcroft Av. Burt —3G **43**
Moordown Clo. Bourn —1A **40**
Moore Av. Bourn —2C **38**
Moore Clo. New M —4F **47**
Moorfield Gro. Bourn —3H **39**
Moorfields Rd. Poole —1B **68**
Moorhills. Wim —5F **13**
Moorings, The. Bourn —6F **39**
Moorings, The. Christ —2D **60**
Moorland Av. New M —5F **47**
Moorland Cres. Poole —6B **34**
Moorland Ga. Ring —6C **6**
Moorland Pde. Poole —6B **34**
Moorland Rd. Bourn —3D **58**
Moorlands Rise. W Moor —4D **8**
Moorlands Rd. Ver —2D **4**
Moorlands Rd. W Moor —5B **8**
Moorland Way. Poole —1B **52**
Moor Rd. Broad —6H **19**
Moors Clo. Hurn —4H **25**
Moorside. St L —1F 17
(off Oak Tree Farm Caravan Pk.)
Moorside Clo. Bourn —2D **38**
Moorside Rd. Bourn —2C **38**
Moorside Rd. Cor M —6D **18**
Moorside Rd. W Moor —5C **8**
Moortown Dri. Wim —3F **21**
Moortown Rd. Ring —6C **6**
Moorvale Rd. Bourn —3A **40**
Moor View Rd. Poole —1C **54**
Morant Rd. Ring —2D **6**
Morden Av. Fern —5A **16**
Morden Rd. Bourn —4G **39**
Moreton Rd. Bourn —1B **40**
Morley Clo. Burt —2G **43**
Morley Rd. Bourn —2G **59**
Mornish Rd. Poole —5B **56**
Morrison Av. Poole —6B **38**
Morris Rd. Poole —5B **36**
Mortimer Clo. Christ —1C **62**
Mortimer Rd. Bourn —4B **40**
Mossley Av. Poole —4B **38**
Motcombe Rd. Poole —5C **56**
Mount Av. New M —4G **47**
Mountbatten Clo. Christ —1C **62**
Mountbatten Dri. Fern —4A **16**
Mountbatten Gdns. Bourn —3F **41**
Mountbatten Rd. Poole & Bourn
—6D **56**
Mount Clo. New M —4G **47**
Mt. Grace Dri. Poole —2G **67**
Mountjoy Clo. Wim —1E **21**
Mt. Pleasant. Ring —4C **6**
Mt. Pleasant Caravan Pk. Hurn
—2H **25**
Mt. Pleasant Dri. Bourn —4F **41**
Mt. Pleasant Dri. Brans —2E **27**
Mt. Pleasant La. Lym —3B **32**
Mt. Pleasant Rd. Poole —4C **54**
Mount Rd. Bourn —1C **38**
Mount Rd. Poole —2F **55**
Mt. Stuart Rd. Bosc —4E **59**
Mount, The. Ring —3E **7**
Mudeford. Christ —2B **62**
Mudeford Farm Caravan Pk. Christ
—2C **62**
Mudeford Grn. Clo. Christ —2B **62**
Mudeford La. Christ —1A **62**
(in two parts)
Mudeford Quay. Christ —3C **62**
Mude Gdns. Christ —2C **62**
Mulberry Gro. Evtn —5H **49**
Mullins Clo. Poole —5E **39**

Munster Rd. Poole —4H **55**
Murley Rd. Bourn —5A **40**
Muscliffe La. Bourn —1A **40**
Muscliffe Rd. Bourn —5H **39**
Myrtle Clo. Hord —1D **48**
Myrtle Rd. Bourn —1C **58**

Nada Rd. Christ —4F **45**
Nairn Rd. Bourn —1G **57**
Nairn Rd. Poole —2A **68**
Naish Holiday Village. New M
—6C **46**
Naish Rd. New M —6D **46**
Namu Rd. Bourn —4G **39**
Nansen Av. Poole —2B **54**
Napier Rd. Poole —4B **52**
Narrow La. Ring —3F **7**
Naseby Rd. Bourn —4A **40**
Nea Clo. Christ —5F **45**
Nea Rd. Christ —5G **45**
Neacroft Clo. New M —5D **46**
Nea Rd. Christ —5G **45**
Needles Point. Mil S —3D **64**
Nelson Clo. New M —2F **47**
Nelson Ct. Poole —5A **54**
Nelson Dri. Christ —1B **62**
Nelson Pl. Lym —2H **51**
Nelson Rd. Poole & Bourn —3C **56**
Netherhall Gdns. Bourn —4E **57**
Netherwood Pl. Cowg —4C **12**
Netley Clo. Poole —6E **37**
Nettleton Clo. Poole —6C **36**
New Borough Rd. Wim —6F **13**
Newbridge Way. Lym —4E **51**
Newbury Dri. Bourn —4F **39**
Newcombe Rd. Bourn —1C **60**
Newcombe Rd. W Moor —5B **8**
Newcroft Gdns. Christ —5E **43**
Newenham Rd. Lym —3G **51**
New Fields Bus. Pk. Poole —5B **36**
Newfoundland Dri. Poole —5A **54**
New Harbour Rd. Poole —6H **53**
New Harbour Rd. E. Poole —6H **53**
New Harbour Rd. S. Poole —6H **53**
New Harbour Rd. W. Poole —6H **53**
Newlands Mnr. Evtn —6H **49**
Newlands Rd. Bourn —1G **59**
Newlands Rd. Christ —6B **44**
Newlands Rd. New M —4H **47**
Newlands Way. Broad —2D **34**
New La. Mil S —3F **65**
New La. New M —5F **29**
Newlyn Way. Poole —6A **38**
Newmans Clo. W Moor —2C **8**
Newman's La. W Moor —3A **8**
New Merrifield. Cole —2H **13**
Newmorton Rd. Bourn —1A **40**
New Orchard. Poole —5H **53**
New Pde. Bourn —2G **39**
New Pk. Rd. Bourn —3A **60**
New Quay Rd. Poole —6H **53**
New Rd. Fern & Bourn —6C **16**
New Rd. Mil S —3G **65**
New Rd. Poole —1H **55**
New Rd. Ring —3H **11**
Newstead Rd. Bourn —3B **60**
New St. Lym —1G **51**
New St. Poole —6H **53**
New St. Ring —5C **6**
Newton Rd. New M —5H **47**
Newton Rd. Poole —1A **68**
Newtown La. Cor M —4D **18**
Newtown La. Ver —4D **4**
Newtown Rd. Ver —3E **5**
New Valley Rd. Mil S —3C **64**
Nicholas Clo. Christ —3B **46**
Nicholas Gdns. Bourn —3E **39**
Nicholson Clo. Poole —5C **36**
Nightingale Clo. Ver —4E **5**
Nightingale La. Poole —5A **54**
Nightjar Clo. Poole —5F **35**
Noble Clo. Bourn —4B **38**
Noel Rd. Bourn —4D **38**
Noon Gdns. Ver —3F **5**
Noon Hill Dri. Ver —3F **5**

Noon Hill Rd. Ver —3F **5**
Norcliffe Clo. Bourn —2D **38**
Norfolk Av. Christ —3D **42**
Norleywood. Christ —5H **45**
Norman Av. Poole —1B **56**
Normandy Clo. Sway —1E **31**
Normandy Dri. Christ —6H **43**
Normandy La. Lym —4G **51**
Normandy Way. Poole —5D **52**
Norman Gdns. Poole —1C **56**
Normanhurst Av. Bourn —4D **40**
Normanton Clo. Christ —4D **42**
Norris Clo. Ashy H —3A **10**
Norris Gdns. New M —4G **47**
Norrish Rd. Poole —2G **55**
North Av. Bourn —5F **23**
Northbourne Av. Bourn —6F **23**
Northbourne Gdns. Bourn —6G **23**
Northbourne Pl. Bourn —6F **23**
Northbrook Rd. Broad —3G **35**
North Clo. Lym —1G **51**
Northcote Rd. Bourn —3B **58**
North Dri. Oss —3E **29**
North Dri. St L —1F 17
(off Oak Tree Farm Caravan Pk.)
North East Ind. Area. Hurn —2E **25**
Northey Rd. Bourn —1C **60**
Northfield Rd. Mil S —3F **65**
Northfield Rd. Ring —2C **6**
N. Greenlands. Lym —3E **51**
North Head. Mil S —2A **64**
Northleigh La. Wim —3G **13**
N. Lodge Rd. Poole —3A **56**
Northmead Dri. Poole —5F **35**
Northmere Dri. Poole —6B **38**
Northmere Rd. Poole —1A **56**
Northover La. Tip —4C **30**
Northover Rd. Lym —1C **50**
N. Poulner Rd. Ring —2D **6**
North Rd. Bourn —2E **59**
North Rd. Ham —5G **53**
North Rd. Poole —3D **54**
North St. Lym —3E **51**
North St. Poole —5A **54**
North West Ind. Area. Hurn
—2C **24**
North Wood. New M —6C **46**
Nortoft Rd. Bourn —1B **58**
Norton Clo. Christ —6H **43**
Norton Rd. Bourn —5G **39**
Norwich Av. Bourn —4F **57**
Norwich Av. W. Bourn —4F **57**
Norwich Ct. Bourn —4F **57**
Norwich Rd. Bourn —4G **57**
Norwood Pl. Bourn —2H **59**
Nouale La. Poul —4F **7**
Noyce Gdns. Bourn —3H **41**
Nuffield Ind. Est. Poole —5A **36**
Nuffield Rd. Poole —6A **36**
Nugent Rd. Bourn —3D **60**
Nursery Av. Bourn —2A **40**
Nursery Rd. Ring —5C **6**
Nursling Grn. Bourn —3D **40**
Nuthatch Clo. Fern —1H **15**
Nuthatch Clo. Poole —6F **35**
Nutley Clo. Bourn —1B **38**
Nutley Way. Bourn —2B **38**

Oak Av. Christ —5B **42**
Oak Clo. Cor M —6C **18**
Oak Clo. W Parl —2G **23**
Oakdale Rd. Poole —1C **54**
Oakdene Clo. Wim —4F **13**
Oakenbrow. Sway —1E **31**
Oakfield Rd. Poole —1A **54**
Oakford Ct. Bourn —2D **40**
Oak Gdns. Evtn —5H **49**
Oakhurst Clo. W Moor —5D **8**
Oakhurst La. W Moor —5D **8**
Oakhurst Rd. W Moor —6D **8**
Oaklands. Lym —3H **51**
Oaklands Clo. Ver —3C **4**
Oakland Wlk. W Parl —2H **23**
Oak La. Ring —3D **6**

A-Z Bournemouth 81

Oakleigh Way. Christ —6H **45**
Oakley Gdns. Uptn —6A **34**
Oakley Hill. Wim —6F **13**
Oakley La. Wim —1B **20**
Oakley Rd. Wim —1B **20**
Oakley Straight. Wim —2C **20**
Oakmead Gdns. Bourn —1A **38**
Oakmead Rd. Poole —5F **35**
Oak Rd. Bourn —1C **58**
Oak Rd. New M —2A **48**
Oak Rd. Poole —1C **52**
Oaks Dri. St L —4H **9**
Oaks, The. Ver —2C **4**
Oaktree Ct. Mil S —3C **64**
Oak Tree Farm Caravan Pk. St L
—1F **17**
Oak Tree Pde. Brans —3D 26
(off Ringwood Rd.)
Oakwood. Bourn —6G **39**
Oakwood Av. New M —1H **47**
Oakwood Clo. Bourn —3B **40**
Oakwood Rd. Bourn —3A **40**
Oakwood Rd. Christ —4G **45**
Oates Rd. Bourn —4G **39**
Oban Rd. Bourn —6G **39**
Okeford Rd. Broad —3A **36**
O.K. Mobile Home Pk. Christ
—5D **44**
Old Barn Clo. Christ —3B **42**
Old Barn Clo. Ring —4E **7**
Old Barn Farm Rd. T Leg —1E **9**
Old Barn Rd. Christ —3B **42**
Old Bound Rd. Poole —1C **52**
Old Bridge Rd. Bourn —5B **42**
Old Christchurch La. Bourn
—4H **57**
Old Christchurch Rd. Bourn
—4H **57**
Old Christchurch Rd. Evtn —4H **49**
Old Coastguard Rd. Poole —5F **67**
Old Farm Clo. Poul —1E **7**
Old Farm Rd. Poole —1C **54**
Old Farm Wlk. Lym —2F **51**
Old Forge Rd. Wim —3F **15**
Old Green Pde. New M —4F **47**
Old Highways M. Wim —5G **13**
Old Kiln Rd. Poole —6D **34**
Old Maltings, The. Lym —1F **51**
Old Manor Clo. Wim —5G **13**
Old Market Rd. Cor M —3A **18**
Old Mill Flats. Ring —5B **6**
Old Milton Grn. New M —4F **47**
Old Milton Rd. New M —4F **47**
Old Orchard. Poole —6A **54**
Old Orchards. Lym —3H **51**
Old Pines Clo. Fern —5C **16**
Old Priory Rd. Bourn —3D **60**
Old Rectory Clo. Cor M —3D **18**
Old Rd. Wim —5D **12**
Old Rope Wlk. Poole —6F **53**
Old Stacks Gdns. Ring —5E **7**
Old Vicarage La. Sway —2G **31**
Old Wareham Rd. Bcn H —3A **34**
Old Wareham Rd. Poole —6E **37**
Oliver Rd. Lym —2F **51**
Olivers Rd. Wim —3A **14**
Olivers Way. Wim —3A **14**
Onslow Gdns. Wim —3F **13**
Ophir Gdns. Bourn —2B **58**
Ophir Rd. Bourn —2B **58**
Oratory Gdns. Poole —1B **68**
Orchard Av. Poole —5D **54**
Orchard Clo. Christ —1E **61**
Orchard Clo. Cor M —4D **18**
Orchard Clo. Fern —4C **16**
Orchard Clo. Ring —3C **6**
Orchard Ct. Ver —4E **5**
Orchard Gro. New M —4G **47**
Orchard La. Cor M —4D **18**
Orchard Leigh. New M —2H **47**
Orchard St. Bourn —4G **57**
Orchard, The. Brans —3C **27**
Orchard, The. Mil S —2D **64**
Orchard Wlk. Bourn —4G 57
(off Commercial Rd.)

Orcheston Rd. Bourn —1B **58**
Orchid Way. Christ —6G **43**
Orford Clo. Christ —1B **42**
Ormonde Rd. Poole —5C **56**
Osborne Ct. Mil S —3C **64**
Osborne Rd. Bourn —5G **39**
Osborne Rd. New M —2G **47**
Osborne Rd. Poole —4F **55**
Osborne Rd. Wim —5F **13**
Osprey Clo. Christ —2C **62**
Ossemsley S. Dri. New M —3E **29**
Oswald Clo. Bourn —3G **39**
Oswald Rd. Bourn —3G **39**
Otter Clo. Poole —1B **52**
Otter Clo. Ver —4E **5**
Otter Rd. Poole —1D **54**
Otters Wlk. New M —5H **29**
Overbury Rd. Poole —4G **55**
Overcombe Clo. Poole —2C **36**
Over Links Dri. Poole —5H **55**
Overstrand Cres. Mil S —4D **64**
Ovington Av. Bourn —6A **42**
Ovington Gdns. Bourn —6A **42**
Owls Clo. New M —4D **58**
Owls Rd. Ver —4E **5**
Oxey Clo. New M —4G **47**
Oxford Av. Bourn —2H **59**
Oxford La. Bourn —5D **22**
Oxford Rd. Bourn —3B **58**
Oxford Ter. Sway —1G **31**

Paddington Clo. Bourn —1H **37**
Paddington Gro. Bourn —2H **37**
Paddock. New M —6C **46**
Paddock Clo. Park —6F **37**
Paddock Clo. St I —3B **10**
Paddock Gdns. Lym —6F **33**
Paddock Gro. Ver —4E **5**
Paddocks, The. Bourn —1F **39**
Paddock, The. St L —1F 17
(off Oak Tree Farm Caravan Pk.)
Padfield Clo. Bourn —1C **60**
Padget Rd. Ring —2E **7**
Paget Clo. Wim —2A **14**
Paget Rd. Bourn —1C **38**
Paisley Rd. Bourn —2A **60**
Palfrey Rd. Bourn —1F **39**
Palma Apartments. New M —6C **46**
Palmer Pl. New M —1F **47**
Palmer Rd. Poole —2A **54**
Palmerston Av. Christ —1H **61**
Palmerston Clo. Poole —6D **34**
Palmerston M. Bourn —2E **59**
Palmerston Rd. Bourn —2E **59**
Palmerston Rd. Park —3H **55**
Palmerston Rd. Uptn —6C **34**
Pamplyn Clo. Lym —1E **51**
Panorama Rd. Poole —6F **67**
Pans Corner. Fern —6D 16
(off Lone Pine Caravan Pk.)
Parade, The. Bourn —4C **60**
Parade, The. Cor M —6D **18**
Parade, The. New M —2B **48**
Parade, The. Wat —4H **35**
Paradise St. Poole —6H **53**
Pardy's Hill. Cor M —3C **18**
Parham Clo. New M —2E **47**
Parham Rd. Bourn —3E **39**
Parish Rd. Poole —4C **54**
Park Av. Bourn —5E **23**
Park Av. Lym —1F **51**
Park Clo. Ashy —6A **30**
Park Clo. Burt —2G **43**
Park Clo. Mil S —3E **65**
Park Ct. Mil S —3C **64**
Park Dri. Ver —2C **4**
Parker Rd. Bourn —6H **39**
Park Gdns. Christ —1H **61**
Park Ga. M. Bourn —4G 57
(off Up. Norwich Rd.)
Park Homer Dri. Wim —2H **13**
Park Homer Rd. Wim —2H **13**
Park Lake Rd. Poole —5C **54**

Parkland Clo. Ver —5H **5**
Parkland Dri. New M —5F **47**
Park La. Bourn —1H **39**
Park La. Mil S —3C **64**
Park La. Wim —5E **13**
Park Pl. Poole —3D **54**
Park Rd. Bourn —2A **58**
Park Rd. Lym —1F **51**
Park Rd. Mil S —3E **65**
Park Rd. New M —4F **47**
Park Rd. New M —6A **30**
Park Rd. Poole —4D **54**
Parkside. Christ —4F **45**
Parkside. Ring —5C **6**
Parkside Gdns. Bourn —3G **39**
Parkside Rd. Poole —3G **55**
Parkstone Av. Poole —3H **55**
Parkstone Heights. Poole —2D **54**
(in two parts)
Parkstone Rd. Poole —4B **54**
Park, The. New M —6C **46**
Park View. Poole —4C **54**
Park View Ct. Bourn —6C **40**
Park Way. W Moor —5B **8**
Parkway Dri. Bourn —5E **41**
Parkwood La. Bourn —2H 59
(off Seabourne Rd.)
Parkwood Rd. Bourn —2G **59**
Parkwood Rd. Wim —5E **13**
Parley Clo. W Parl —2H **23**
Parley La. Parl —3B **24**
Parley Rd. Bourn —3A **40**
Parmiter Dri. Wim —5G **13**
Parmiter Rd. Wim —5G **13**
Parmiter Way. Wim —5G **13**
Parr St. Poole —3E **55**
Parsonage Barn La. Ring —3C **6**
Parsonage Rd. Bourn —4A **58**
Partridge Clo. Christ —2C **62**
Partridge Dri. Poole —6F **55**
Partridge Grn. New M —5H **29**
Partridge Wlk. Poole —6G **55**
Pascoe Clo. Poole —3E **55**
Passford Hill. Lym —4F **33**
Patchins Rd. Poole —3B **52**
(in two parts)
Pauls La. Sway —3H **31**
Pauncefote Rd. Bourn —2G **59**
Pauntley Rd. Christ —1A **62**
Pavan Gdns. Bourn —3E **39**
Payne Clo. W Moor —2C **8**
Peace Clo. Brans —3C **26**
Pearce Av. Poole —6E **55**
Pearce Gdns. Poole —6E **55**
Pearce Rd. Poole —1B **52**
Pearl Gdns. Bourn —1E **39**
Pearl Rd. Bourn —1E **39**
Pearman Dri. Lym —3G **51**
Pearson Av. Poole —2F **55**
Pearson Gdns. Bourn —5F **23**
Pear Tree Clo. Brans —3D **26**
Peartree Ct. Lym —3G **51**
Peckham Av. New M —3G **47**
Peddlars Wlk. Ring —4B **6**
Peel Clo. Poole —2G **55**
Peel Ct. Christ —1D **60**
Pegasus Av. Hord —3E **49**
Pegasus Ct. New M —2G 47
(off Spencer Rd.)
Pelham Clo. Christ —1H **61**
Pelican Mead. High —5E **7**
Pembroke Rd. Bourn —5D **56**
Pembroke Rd. Poole —6H **37**
Penelope Ct. Christ —6B **46**
Pengelly Av. Bourn —6G **23**
Pennant Way. Christ —6B **44**
Penn Clo. New M —4E **47**
Penn Ct. W Moor —5B **8**
Penn Hill Av. Poole —4H **55**
Pennine Way. Ver —4D **4**
Pennington Clo. Lym —3E **51**
Pennington Clo. W Moor —6B **8**
Pennington Cres. W Moor —5B **8**
Pennington Oval. Lym —3D **50**
Pennington Rd. W Moor —5B **8**

Penny Hedge. New M —5H **47**
Penny La. Bourn —3E 59
(off Royal Arc.)
Penny's Wlk. Fern —5B **8**
Penny Way. Christ —1E **63**
Pennywell Gdns. New M —1B **48**
Penrith Clo. Ver —4C **4**
Penrith Rd. Bourn —3G **59**
Penrose Rd. Fern —3B **16**
Percy Rd. Bourn —3E **59**
Peregrine Rd. Christ —1C **62**
Pergin Cres. Poole —6H **35**
Pergin Way. Poole —6H **35**
Perryfield Gdns. Bourn —5H **41**
Perry Gdns. Poole —6A **54**
Persley Rd. Bourn —1F **39**
Perth Clo. Christ —4C **42**
Peters Clo. Poole —1C **52**
Peters Dri. Fern —6D 16
(off Lone Pine Caravan Pk.)
Petersfield Pl. Bourn —6H **41**
Petersfield Rd. Bourn —1G **59**
(in two parts)
Petersham Rd. Poole —5F **35**
Petit Rd. Bourn —2A **40**
Petwyn Clo. Fern —3E **17**
Peverell Rd. Poole —3B **52**
Peveril Clo. Ashy H —1B **10**
Phelipps Rd. Cor M —4D **18**
Phyldon Clo. Poole —2F **55**
Phyldon Rd. Poole —1F **55**
Pickard Rd. Fern —2D **16**
Pickering Clo. Broad —3G **35**
Pickford Rd. Bourn —4G **39**
Pier App. Bourn —5H **57**
Pig Shoot La. Hurn —1F **41**
Pilford Heath Rd. Wim —2A **14**
Pilgrim's Clo. New M —1A **48**
Pilgrims Pk. Ring —3E **7**
Pilgrims Way. Poole —6G **35**
Pilley Hill. Pill —2G **33**
Pilley St. Pill —2H **33**
Pilot Hight Rd. Bourn —1C **38**
Pilsdon Dri. Poole —2C **36**
Pimpern Clo. Poole —3C **36**
Pine Av. Bourn —3A **60**
Pine Av. Poole —6B **38**
Pinebeach Ct. Park —1C **68**
Pinecliffe Av. Bourn —3A **60**
Pinecliffe Rd. New M —6C **46**
Pinecliff Rd. Poole —1C **68**
Pine Clo. Fern —2A **16**
Pine Clo. New M —5E **47**
Pine Cres. Christ —6G **45**
Pine Dri. Poole —4B **56**
(in two parts)
Pine Dri. St I —3B **10**
Pine Dri. E. Poole —5C **56**
Pine End. Fern —6D 16
(off Lone Pine Caravan Pk.)
Pine Glen Av. Fern —1A **16**
Pineholt Clo. St I —2C **10**
Pinehurst. Mil S —3C **64**
Pinehurst Av. Christ —2B **62**
Pinehurst Pk. W Moor —1D **16**
Pinehurst Rd. W Moor —6C **8**
Pine Mnr. Rd. Ashy H —2H **9**
Pine Rd. Bourn —4H **39**
Pine Rd. Cor M —2F **19**
Pinesprings Dri. Broad —3E **35**
Pinetops Clo. Lym —2D **50**
Pine Tree Clo. Wim —4F **13**
Pine Tree Glen. Bourn —4E **57**
Pine Tree Wlk. Poole —5F **35**
Pine Vale Cres. Bourn —2G **39**
Pine View Clo. Poole —1C **52**
Pine View Clo. Ver —2B **4**
Pine View Rd. Ver —2B **4**
Pine Wlk. Ver —4F **5**
Pinewood Av. Bourn —6F **23**
Pinewood Clo. Bourn —6F **23**
Pinewood Clo. Christ —3A **46**
Pinewood Clo. Poole —6A **34**
Pinewood Gdns. Fern —2B **16**
Pinewood Rd. Brnk P —6D **56**

Pinewood Rd. Christ —4H 45
Pinewood Rd. Fern —1A 16
Pinewood Rd. Hord —2C 48
Pinewood Rd. St I —3B 10
Pinewood Rd. W. Poole —6A 34
Pipers Ash. Ring —3E 7
Pipers Dri. Christ —6C 44
Pipin Clo. Lym —3G 51
Pippin Clo. Christ —3C 42
Pitmore La. Sway —1G 31
Pittmore Rd. Burt —3G 43
Pitts Pl. New M —3B 48
Pitwines Clo. Poole —5B 54
Plantaganet Cres. Bourn —6H 21
Plantation. Evtn —5A 50
Plantation Ct. Poole —4A 36
Plantation Dri. Christ —3A 46
Plantation Rd. Poole —4A 36
Plant Pk. Rd. Ring —4E 11
Plassey Cres. Bourn —6E 23
Platoff Rd. Lym —5G 51
Playfields Dri. Poole —1A 56
Pleasance Way. New M —2F 47
Plecy Clo. W Parl —6B 16
Plemont Clo. Poole —4A 38
Pless Rd. Mil S —2A 64
Plover Dri. Mil S —3F 65
Plumer Rd. Poole —4G 35
Poles La. Lym —4G 51
Policemans La. Poole —6A 34
Pomona Clo. Fern —3B 16
Pompey's La. Wim & Fern —5G 15
Pond Clo. New M —2G 47
Ponsonby Rd. Poole —3H 55
Pony Dri. Uptn —6D 34
Poole Commerce Cen. Poole
                        —2B 56
Poole Hill. Bourn —4F 57
Poole La. Bourn —2A 38
Poole Rd. Bourn —3D 56
Poole Rd. Brnk —3B 56
Poole Rd. Uptn —6C 34
Poole Rd. Wim —5E 13
Popes Rd. Poole —1B 54
Poplar Clo. Brans —3E 27
Poplar Clo. Christ —5B 46
Poplar Clo. Poole —6H 53
(off Levet's La.)
Poplar Clo. Wim —4F 13
Poplar Cres. Ring —4D 6
Poplar La. Brans —2E 27
Poplar Rd. New M —1B 48
Poplar Way. Ring —4D 6
Poppy Clo. Christ —5D 44
Portarlington Clo. Bourn —5F 57
Portarlington Rd. Bourn —4E 57
Portchester Pl. Bourn —2B 58
Portchester Rd. Bourn —1A 58
Portelet Clo. Poole —3H 37
Porter Rd. Poole —6H 35
Porters La. Wim —3C 14
Portesham Gdns. Bourn —1B 40
Portesham Way. Poole —2C 36
Portfield Clo. Christ —5E 43
Portfield Rd. Christ —6D 42
Portland Rd. Bourn —4A 40
Portman Cres. Bourn —3H 59
Portman Rd. Bourn —2F 59
Portman Ter. Bourn —3H 59
Portswood Dri. Bourn —1A 40
Port View Caravan Pk. Hurn
                        —1H 25
Post Office La. Poole —5A 54
(off High St. Poole)
Post Office La. St I —2C 10
Post Office Rd. Bourn —4H 57
Potterne Way. T Leg —5E 5
Potters Way. Poole —5G 55
Pottery Rd. Poole —5E 55
Poulner Mobile Home Pk. Ring
                        —1E 7
Poulner Pk. Ring —2E 7
Pound Clo. Poole —2D 54
Pound Clo. Ring —3C 6
Pound La. Christ —1F 61

Pound La. Poole —2C 54
Pound Rd. Lym —3D 50
Powell Rd. Poole —4F 55
Powerscourt Rd. New M —6D 46
Powis Clo. New M —2H 47
Powlett Rd. Lym —2G 51
Preston La. Burt —2H 43
Preston Rd. Poole —1A 54
Preston Way. Christ —5F 45
Prestwood Clo. New M —4F 47
Priestlands La. Lym —2E 51
Priestlands Pl. Lym —2F 51
Priestlands Rd. Lym —2E 51
Priestley Rd. Bourn —4D 38
Primrose Gdns. Poole —4F 35
Primrose Way. Christ —5E 45
Primrose Way. Cor M —4E 19
Prince of Wales Rd. Bourn —3D 56
Princes Pl. New M —1A 48
Princes Rd. Fern —4B 16
Princess Av. Christ —1F 61
Princess Rd. Poole & Bourn
(in two parts)   —3C 56
Pringles Clo. Fern —4C 16
Pringles Dri. Fern —4C 16
Priors Clo. Christ —6E 45
Priors Rd. Poole —5F 35
Priors Wlk. Wim —4D 12
Priory Gdns. W Moor —1E 17
Priory Ind. Pk. Christ —6D 44
Priory Quay. Christ —2G 61
Priory Rd. Bourn —5G 57
Priory Rd. W Moor —1E 17
Priory View Pl. Bourn —2A 40
Priory View Rd. Bourn —2A 40
Priory View Rd. Burt —3G 43
Privet Rd. Bourn —5G 39
Promenade. Can C —4A 68
Promenade. Christ —2D 62
Promenade. Ham —6E 53
Promenade. Poole —5G 67
Prosperous St. Poole —5A 54
Prunus Clo. Fern —2H 15
Prunus Dri. Fern —2H 15
Puddletown Cres. Poole —3D 36
Pullman Ct. W Moor —5B 8
Pullman Way. Ring —5C 6
Purbeck Av. Poole —6E 53
Purbeck Clo. Poole —6B 34
Purbeck Dri. Ver —4D 4
Purbeck Gdns. Poole —2D 54
Purbeck Rd. Bourn —4G 57
Purbeck Rd. New M —6D 46
Purchase Rd. Poole —6D 38
Purewell. Christ —1H 61
Purewell Clo. Christ —1A 62
Purewell Cross. Christ —1A 62
Purewell Cross Rd. Christ —6H 43
Purewell M. Christ —1H 61
Pussex La. Hurn —3G 25
Pye La. Cor M —4D 18

Quarry Clo. Wim —2B 14
Quarry Dri. Wim —2B 14
Quarry Rd. Wim —2B 14
Quay Hill. Lym —1H 51
Quayle Dri. Bourn —5B 22
Quay Rd. Christ —1F 61
Quay Rd. Lym —1H 51
Quay St. Lym —1H 51
Quay, The. Christ —2G 61
Quay, The. Poole —6H 53
Queen Anne Dri. Wim —3B 20
Queen Elizabeth Av. Lym —1F 51
Queen Katherine Rd. Lym —2H 51
Queen Mary Av. Bourn —3H 39
Queens Av. Christ —2F 61
Queens Clo. W Moor —6B 8
Queens Ct. Bourn —5B 40
Queen's Gdns. Bourn —3F 57
Queens Gro. New M —1A 48
Queensland Rd. Bourn —2G 59
Queens M. Lym —2F 51
Queensmount. Bourn —6C 40

Queen's Pk. Av. Bourn —5B 40
Queens Pk. Gdns. Bourn —6C 40
Queens Pk. Rd. Bourn —6D 40
Queens Pk. S. Dri. Bourn —6D 40
Queens Pk. W. Dri. Bourn —6C 40
Queens Rd. Bourn —4F 57
Queen's Rd. Christ —1A 62
Queen's Rd. Cor M —6D 18
Queens Rd. Fern —2B 16
Queens Rd. Poole —3H 55
Queen St. Lym —2F 51
Queensway. New M —2E 47
Queens Way. Ring —4D 6
Queenswood Av. Bourn —4E 41
Queenswood Dri. Fern —2B 16
Quince La. Wim —4G 13
Quintin Clo. Christ —5H 45
Quomp. Ring —4C 6

Radipole Rd: Poole —3E 37
Raglan Gdns. Bourn —3C 38
Railway Ter. Hint —3G 45
Raleigh Clo. Christ —2B 62
Raleigh Clo. New M —2F 47
Raleigh Clo. Ring —3E 7
Raleigh Rd. Poole —4A 38
Ralph Rd. Cor M —4D 18
Ramley Rd. Lym —1C 50
Rampart, The. Lym —6F 33
Ramsey Ct. Christ —1D 60
Randalls Hill. Ly Min —4A 34
Randolph Rd. Bourn —3E 59
Randolph Rd. Poole —2G 55
Ranelagh Rd. Christ —6H 45
Ravenscourt Rd. Bourn —2A 60
Ravenscourt Rd. Lym —2F 51
Ravensdale Clo. Poole —1G 55
Ravens Way. Mil S —3D 64
Ravenswood Pk. Caravan Site. Ring
                        —6H 7
Raven Way. Christ —2C 62
Ravine Rd. Bourn —3H 59
Ravine Rd. Poole —1B 68
Raymond Clo. Ver —3F 5
Raynards Ct. Poole —4D 54
Rebbeck Rd. Bourn —1G 59
Recreation Rd. Poole —1H 55
Rectory Av. Cor M —2D 18
Rectory Rd. Poole —1A 54
Redan Clo. Christ —6H 45
Redbreast Rd. Bourn —2A 40
Redbreast Rd. N. Bourn —2A 40
Redcliffe Clo. Burt —3G 43
Redcotts La. Wim —4D 12
(in two parts)
Redcotts Rd. Wim —4D 12
Redhill Av. Bourn —3G 39
Redhill Clo. Poole —2G 39
Redhill Ct. Bourn —1H 39
Redhill Cres. Bourn —2H 39
Redhill Dri. Bourn —3G 39
Redhoave Rd. Poole —3C 36
Redhorn Clo. Poole —3C 52
Redlands. Poole —2B 56
Red La. Cor M —3A 18
Red Oaks Clo. Fern —2H 15
Redshank Clo. Poole —4F 35
Redvers Clo. Lym —3F 51
Redvers Rd. Christ —6A 44
Redwood Clo. Lym —6E 33
Redwood Clo. Ring —4D 6
Redwood Dri. Fern —1A 16
Redwood Rd. Poole —5A 34
Regent Dri. Bourn —5F 41
Regent Way. Christ —1F 61
Reid St. Christ —6E 43
Rempstone Rd. Wim —2B 20
Renault Dri. Broad —4G 35
Renouf Clo. Lym —2E 51
Retreat Rd. Wim —5F 13
Rhinefield Rd. New M —1E 29
Rhiners Clo. Sway —1F 31
Ribble Clo. Broad —3G 35

Ricardo Cres. Christ —1C 62
Rice Gdns. Poole —3D 52
Rice Ter. Poole —3D 52
Richard Clo. Poole —5B 34
Richmond Ct. Mil S —3C 64
Richmond Ct. New M —2G 47
(off Spencer Rd.)
Richmond Gdns. Bourn —4H 57
Richmond Hill. Bourn —4H 57
Richmond Hill Dri. Bourn —4H 57
Richmond Pk. Av. Bourn —6B 40
Richmond Pk. Clo. Bourn —1D 58
Richmond Pk. Cres. Bourn —6C 40
Richmond Pk. Rd. Bourn —6B 40
Richmond Rd. Poole —2G 55
Richmond Rd. Wim —5F 13
Richmond Wood Rd. Bourn
                        —6B 40
Ridgefield Gdns. Christ —5F 45
Ridgemount Gdns. Poole —4E 53
Ridgeway. Broad —1H 35
Ridgeway. Cor M —3D 18
Ridge Way. W Parl —3G 23
Ridgeway La. Lym —3F 51
Ridley Rd. Bourn —5H 39
Ridout Clo. Bourn —4D 38
Riggs Gdns. Bourn —3B 38
Rigler Rd. Poole —6G 53
Ringbury. Lym —5F 33
Ringwood Rd. Ashy H —6F 9
Ringwood Rd. Bourn & Fern
                        —3H 37
Ringwood Rd. Brans —2C 26
Ringwood Rd. Christ —1G 45
Ringwood Rd. Poole —3D 54
Ringwood Rd. T Leg —2A 8
Ringwood Rd. Ver —2D 4
Ringwood Rd. Service Rd. Ashy H
                        —4B 10
Ringwood Rd. S. Poole —5F 37
Ringwood Trading Est. Ring —5C 6
Ripon Rd. Bourn —5A 40
Ritchie Pl. W Moor —3B 8
Ritchie Rd. Bourn —1D 38
River Clo. Wim —3E 13
Riverdale La. Christ —1E 61
River Gdns. Mil S —3E 65
Riverlea Rd. Christ —1E 61
Rivermead Gdns. Christ —3C 42
Riversdale Rd. Bourn —3E 61
Riverside. Bourn —1H 59
Riverside. Ring —5B 6
Riverside Av. Bourn —3H 41
Riverside Bus. Pk. Lym —1H 51
Riverside La. Bourn —2D 60
Riverside Pk. Christ —2E 61
Riverside Pk. Ind. Est. Wim —5F 13
Riverside Rd. Bourn —2D 60
Riverside Rd. W Moor —5A 8
Rivers Reach. Lym —2H 51
River Way. Christ —4B 42
R. L. Stevenson Av. Bourn —4D 56
Roberts Clo. Evtn —4A 50
Roberts La. Bourn —1G 59
Roberts Rd. Poole —4H 35
Robin Cres. New M —6D 28
Robin Gro. New M —3F 47
Robins Way. Christ —2D 62
Robinswood Dri. Fern —1B 16
Robsall Clo. Poole —6A 38
Rochester Rd. Bourn —1D 38
Rockbourne Gdns. New M —5D 46
Rockford Clo. Bourn —4D 60
Rockley Caravan Pk. Poole —4B 52
Rockley Rd. Poole —5E 53
Rodbourne Clo. Evtn —5H 49
Rodney Clo. Poole —5C 38
Rodney Ct. Poole —6A 54
Rodney Dri. Christ —1B 62
Rodway. Wim —5E 13
Rodwell Clo. Bourn —5E 23
Roebuck Clo. New M —2F 47
Roeshot Cres. Christ —4G 45
Roeshot Hill. Christ —4E 45
Rolls Dri. Bourn —3F 61

Roman Heights. Cor M —3E 19
Roman Rd. Broad & Cor M —6E 19
Roman Rd. Poole —5E 35
Romney Clo. Bourn —2G 39
Romney Rd. Bourn —1G 39
Rookcliff. Mil S —3C 64
Rookcliff Way. Mil S —3C 64
Rookes La. Lym —3F 51
Rook Hill Rd. Christ —1D 62
Roosevelt Cres. Bourn —5D 22
Rope Hill. Bold —2E 33
Ropers La. Poole —6D 34
Ropley Rd. Bourn —6A 42
Rosamund Av. Wim —2C 20
Roscrea Clo. Bourn —3F 61
Roscrea Dri. Bourn —3F 61
Rosebery Clo. Ver —4G 5
Rosebery Rd. Bourn —2G 59
Rosebud Av. Bourn —3A 40
Rose Cres. Poole —1D 54
Rosedale Clo. Christ —1A 62
Rose Gdns. Bourn —3H 39
Rosehill Clo. Brans —2D 26
Rosehill Dri. Brans —2C 26
Rosemary Gdns. Poole —6F 37
Rosemary Rd. Poole —6F 37
Rosemount Rd. Bourn —5D 56
Rosewood Gdns. New M —1F 47
Roslin Rd. Bourn —6G 39
Roslin Rd. S. Bourn —6F 39
Ross Gdns. Bourn —6G 21
Ross Glades. Bourn —1G 57
Rossley Clo. Christ —3G 45
Rossmore Dri. Ver —3C 4
Rossmore Rd. Poole —5G 37
Ross Rd. Ring —1E 7
Rotary Clo. Wim —2H 13
Rothbury Pk. New M —3H 47
Rotherfield Rd. Bourn —4H 59
Rotherfield Rd. Christ —4A 46
Rothesay Dri. Christ —6G 45
Rothesay Rd. Bourn —1E 57
Rotterdam Dri. Christ —6H 43
Roumelia La. Bourn —3E 59
Roundhaye Rd. Bourn —6B 22
Roundways. Bourn —2B 38
Rowan Clo. Christ —5F 45
Rowan Clo. St L —3H 9
Rowan Clo. Sway —2F 31
Rowan Dri. Christ —5F 45
Rowan Dri. Poole —4E 35
Rowan Dri. Ver —5F 5
Rowans Pk. Lym —2F 51
Rowbarrow Clo. Poole —3C 36
Rowena Rd. Bourn —2D 60
Rowland Av. Poole —1C 54
Rowlands Hill. Wim —4E 13
Rownhams Rd. Bourn —2C 40
Royal Arc. Bourn —3E 59
Royal Oak Rd. Bourn —6E 23
Royden La. Bold —1F 33
Royston Dri. Wim —4F 13
Royston Pl. New M —5H 47
Rozelle Rd. Poole —3G 55
Rubens Clo. New M —2H 47
Rufford Gdns. Bourn —2C 60
Rugby Rd. Poole —4G 35
Runnymede Av. Bourn —5H 21
Runton Rd. Poole —2B 56
Runway, The. Christ —6D 44
Rushall La. Cor M —1A 34
Rushcombe Way. Cor M —5D 18
Rushford Warren. Christ —2B 62
Rushmere Rd. Bourn —6A 42
Rushton Cres. Bourn —1H 57
Ruskin Av. Bourn —2B 40
Russell Cotes Rd. Bourn —5A 58
Russell Dri. Christ —1H 61
Russell Gdns. Poole —3C 52
Russell Gdns. St I —2D 10
Russel Rd. Bourn —5E 23
Russet Clo. Fern —3B 16
Russett Clo. Lym —3H 51
Rutland Rd. Bourn —5B 40
Rutland Rd. Christ —4D 42

Ryall Rd. Poole —4B 36
Ryan Clo. Fern —2A 16
Ryan Gdns. Bourn —5D 22
Ryan Gdns. Fern —2A 16
Rydal Clo. Christ —1B 42
Ryecroft Av. Bourn —6A 22

Saddle Clo. Wim —3C 14
Saffron Dri. Christ —5D 44
St Albans Av. Bourn —6B 40
St Albans Cres. Bourn —5B 40
St Albans Rd. Bourn —6B 40
St Aldhelms. Poole —3A 56
St Aldhelm's Clo. Poole —4B 56
St Aldhelm's Rd. Poole —3B 56
St Andrews. Christ —1E 61
St Andrews Rd. Broad —6G 19
St Anne's Av. Bourn —2C 60
St Annes Gdns. Lym —2F 51
St Anne's Rd. Poole —6B 34
St Ann's Ct. Bourn —2E 59
St Anthony's Rd. Bourn —2H 57
St Aubyn's Ct. Poole —5H 53
St Aubyns La. Hang —2G 7
St Augustin's Rd. Bourn —2H 57
St Brelades Av. Poole —3H 37
St Catherines. Wim —5E 13
St Catherine's Hill La. Christ
—3D 42
St Catherine's Pde. Christ —4D 42
St Catherine's Path. Bourn —4C 60
St Catherine's Rd. Bourn —4C 60
St Catherine's Way. Christ —2B 42
St Clair Rd. Poole —3A 68
St Clements Gdns. Bourn —2D 58
St Clements La. Poole —6H 53
St Clements Rd. Bourn —2D 58
St Clements Rd. Poole —6E 37
St David's Ct. Bourn —2E 59
St David's Rd. Poole —5B 34
St Denys. New M —4H 47
St George's Av. Bourn —5C 40
St Georges Av. Poole —5F 37
St George's Clo. Bourn —5C 40
St Georges Clo. Christ —5F 45
St George's Ct. Bourn —2E 59
St Georges Dri. Brans —3D 26
St Georges Dri. Fern —5A 16
St Helier Rd. Poole —4H 37
St Ives End La. St I —3C 10
St Ives Gdns. Bourn —2H 57
St Ives Pk. Ashy H —2C 10
St Ives Wood. St I —2D 10
St James Clo. Poole —6H 53
St James Rd. Fern —3G 15
St James Rd. Sway —1G 31
St James Sq. Bourn —2G 59
St John's Clo. Wim —5F 13
St John's Ct. Bourn —2E 59
St John's Hill. Wim —4F 13
St Johns Rd. Bourn —3E 59
St John's Rd. Christ —1D 60
St Johns Rd. New M —4G 29
St Johns Rd. Poole —3B 54
St Just Clo. Fern —6H 15
St Ledger's Pl. Bourn —1D 58
St Ledger's Rd. Bourn —1D 58
St Leonard's Rd. Bourn —1B 58
St Leonards Way. Ashy H —2H 9
St Luke's Rd. Bourn —6H 39
St Margaret's Av. Christ —1E 61
St Margarets Clo. Wim —4C 12
St Margaret's Hill. Wim —3C 12
St Margaret's Rd. Bourn —3D 38
St Margaret's Rd. Poole —3B 54
St Marks Rd. Bourn —2D 38
St Marks Rd. Lym —2D 50
St Martins Rd. Uptn —6A 34
St Mary Gro. Hord —3E 49
St Mary's Clo. Brans —3E 27
St Mary's Rd. Bourn —1D 58
St Mary's Rd. Fern —4B 16
St Mary's Rd. Poole —4B 54
St Merrin's Clo. Bourn —1E 39

St Michaels Clo. Ver —4D 4
St Michael's Pl. Bourn —4G 57
(off St Michael's Rd.)
St Michael's Rd. Bourn —4G 57
St Michael's Rd. Ver —4D 4
St Osmunds Rd. Poole —3G 55
St Paul's La. Bourn —3B 58
St Paul's Pl. Bourn —3B 58
St Paul's Rd. Bourn —3A 58
St Peter's Cres. Bourn —4H 57
St Peter's Rd. Bourn —4H 57
St Peter's Rd. Poole —3E 55
St Peter's Wlk. Bourn —4H 57
(off Old Christchurch Rd.)
St Saviours Clo. Bourn —6A 42
Saints Clo. T Leg —2A 8
St Stephen's La. Ver —3E 5
St Stephen's Rd. Bourn —3G 57
St Stephen's Way. Bourn —3H 57
St Swithun's Rd. Bourn —3B 58
St Swithun's Rd. S. Bourn —3B 58
St Thomas Clo. Bourn —3F 39
St Thomas Pk. Lym —2F 51
St Thomas St. Lym —2F 51
St Valerie Rd. Bourn —2H 57
St Winifred's Rd. Bourn —2H 57
Salerno Pl. Poole —5D 52
Salisbury Rd. Bourn —3E 59
Salisbury Rd. Poole —2G 55
Salisbury Rd. Ring —3B 6
Salisbury Rd. Wink —1G 43
Salterns Ct. Poole —1F 67
Salterns Rd. Poole —4E 55
Salterns Way. Poole —1F 67
Salter Rd. Poole —6G 67
Saltgrass La. Key —5G 65
Saltings Rd. Poole —1B 52
Samber Clo. Lym —1E 51
Samphire Clo. Lym —6G 33
Samples Way. Poole —5D 36
Samson Rd. Poole —4D 52
Sancreed Rd. Poole —6A 38
Sandbanks Rd. Poole —4D 54
Sandbourne Rd. Bourn —6E 57
Sandbourne Rd. Poole —3B 54
Sandecotes Rd. Poole —3G 55
Sanderlings. High —5E 7
Sandford Clo. Bourn —2C 40
Sandford Way. Broad —3F 35
Sandhills Caravan Pk. Christ
—2D 62
Sandhills Clo. Poole —3B 36
Sandmartin Clo. New M —4F 47
Sandown Rd. Christ —1A 62
Sandpiper Clo. Poole —4F 35
Sandpit La. Poole —4B 54
Sandringham Clo. Bourn —1B 40
Sandringham Gdns. Bourn —1B 40
Sandringham Rd. Poole —4F 55
Sandy Clo. Wim —1A 14
Sandyhurst Clo. Poole —4A 36
Sandy La. Bourn —2H 59
Sandy La. Christ —3C 42
Sandy La. Poole —1A 52
Sandy La. St I —3B 10
Sandy La. T Leg —1A 8
Sandy La. Ver —3E 5
Sandy La. Wim —1A 14
Sandy Mead Rd. Bourn —4F 41
Sandy Plot. Burt —4G 43
Sandy Way. Bourn —2G 39
(in two parts)
San Remo Towers. Bosc —4E 59
Saracen Clo. Lym —4E 51
Sarah Clo. Bourn —5H 41
Sarah Sands Clo. Christ —5H 43
Sark Rd. Poole —5H 37
Sarum Ct. W Moor —3C 8
(in two parts)
Sarum St. Poole —6H 53
Sarum Wlk. Lym —5F 33
Saulfland Dri. Christ —5F 45
Saulfland Pl. Christ —5F 45
Saxonbury Rd. Bourn —1C 60
Saxon Cen. Christ —6F 43

Saxonford Rd. Christ —6E 45
Saxonhurst Clo. Bourn —6G 23
Saxonhurst Rd. Bourn —1F 39
Saxon King Gdns. Bourn —3F 61
Saxon Pl. Lym —5F 33
Saxon Sq. Christ —1F 61
Scarf Rd. Poole —5D 36
School Clo. Lym —2E 51
School La. Bourn —6D 22
School La. Lym —1G 51
School La. Mil S —1E 65
School La. Pill —2H 33
School La. Ring —4C 6
School La. St I —2C 10
School La. Wim —4D 12
Scott Clo. Poole —4B 38
Scotter Rd. Bourn —1H 59
Scott Rd. Poole —4B 38
Scott's Grn. Christ —5B 44
Scotts Hills La. Christ —6H 43
Seabourne Pl. Bourn —2H 59
Seabourne Rd. Bourn —2G 59
Seabreeze Way. Mil S —1A 64
Seacombe Rd. Poole —6F 67
Seacroft Av. New M —5E 47
Seafield Clo. New M —6F 47
Seafield Dri. Bourn —2C 60
Seafield Rd. Bourn —3B 60
Seafield Rd. Christ —1E 63
Seafield Rd. New M —5E 47
Seagull Rd. Bourn —4C 40
Seamoor La. Bourn —4D 56
Seamoor Rd. Bourn —4D 56
Sea Pines. Mil S —3C 64
Sea Rd. Bosc —4E 59
Sea Rd. Mil S —3E 65
Sea Rd. New M —5E 47
Sea Rd. S'brne —4D 60
Seaton Clo. Christ —5B 44
Seaton Clo. Lym —6G 33
Seaton Rd. Christ —5B 46
Seatown Clo. Poole —4E 37
Sea View Rd. Christ —4C 46
Sea View Rd. New M —6C 46
Sea View Rd. Park —2E 55
Sea View Rd. Uptn —6A 34
Sea Vixen Ind. Est. Christ —6C 44
Seaward Av. Bourn —3H 59
Seaward Av. New M —6E 47
Seaward Path. Poole —1C 68
Seaway. New M —5H 47
Seaway Av. Christ —6E 45
Seawinds. Mil S —2A 64
Second Marine Av. New M —6G 47
Sedgley Rd. Bourn —5G 39
Selby Clo. Broad —2G 35
Seldown Bri. Poole —5B 54
Seldown La. Poole —4B 54
Seldown Rd. Poole —5B 54
Selfridge Av. Bourn —4F 61
Selfridge Clo. Bourn —4F 61
Self Rd. Poole —5G 53
Seliot Clo. Poole —2B 54
Selkirk Clo. Wim —2C 20
Sellwood Way. New M —5D 46
Selwood Caravan Pk. Bourn
—4E 23
Selworthy Clo. Poole —5E 55
Serpentine La. Poole —4A 54
Serpentine Rd. Poole —4A 54
Setley Gdns. Bourn —2E 41
Set Thorns Rd. Sway —1G 31
Sevenoaks Dri. Bourn —6G 41
Severn Rd. Fern —3E 17
Seymour Rd. Ring —2D 6
Shackleton Sq. Brans —2D 26
Shaftesbury Clo. W Moor —5D 8
Shaftesbury Rd. Bourn —1C 58
Shaftesbury Rd. Poole —4B 54
Shaftesbury Rd. W Moor —6D 8
Shakespeare Rd. Bourn —6B 42
Shakespeare Rd. Wim —3E 13
Shallow La. Lym —3F 33
Shamrock Ct. Wim —5E 13
Shapland Av. Bourn —6A 22

Shapwick Rd. Poole —6G **53**
Shard Clo. Ver —3E **5**
Sharlands Clo. Broad —2H **35**
Sharp Rd. Poole —6C **38**
Sharvells Rd. Mil S —2C **64**
Shaves La. New M —6G **29**
Shawford Gdns. Bourn —3D **40**
Shawford Rd. Bourn —2D **40**
Shaw Rd. Ring —1E **7**
Shears Brook Clo. Brans —2D **26**
Shelbourne Clo. Bourn —1C **58**
Shelbourne Rd. Bourn —1B **58**
Sheldrake Gdns. Hord —2F **49**
Sheldrake Rd. Christ —2C **62**
Shelley Clo. Ashy H —2H **9**
Shelley Clo. Bourn —2E **59**
Shelley Clo. Christ —6E **45**
Shelley Gdns. Bourn —2E **59**
Shelley Hill. Christ —6F **45**
Shelley Rd. Bourn —2E **59**
Shelley Rd. Poole —2H **55**
Shelley Rd. E. Bourn —2F **59**
Shelley Way. Mil S —2D **64**
Shelton Rd. Bourn —1A **60**
Shepherd Clo. Christ —4H **45**
Shepherds Way. Bourn —6G **41**
Sheppards Field. Wim —3D **12**
Sherborn Cres. Poole —4D **53**
Sherborne Dri. Fern —5B **16**
Sherfield Clo. Bourn —3D **40**
Sheringham Rd. Poole —2B **56**
Sherrin Clo. Poole —2B **54**
Sherwood Av. Fern —6A **16**
Sherwood Av. Poole —5D **54**
Sherwood Clo. Christ —6D **42**
Sherwood Dri. Ver —3F **5**
Shillingstone Dri. Bourn —1B **40**
Shillito Rd. Poole —2H **55**
Shingle Bank Dri. Mil S —3D **64**
Shipstal Clo. Poole —3C **52**
Shires Copse. Bourn —4D **60**
Shirley Clo. Brans —2D **26**
Shirley Clo. W Moor —5C **8**
Shirley Holms. Lym —2A **32**
Shirley Rd. Bourn —4A **40**
Shirley Rd. Park —1F **55**
Shore Av. Poole —1C **52**
Shore Clo. Mil S —3D **64**
Shore Clo. Poole —1C **52**
Shorefield Caravan Pk. Mil S
—6E **49**
Shorefield Cres. Mil S —2C **64**
Shorefield Rd. Down —1A **64**
Shorefield Way. Mil S —2C **64**
Shore Gdns. Poole —1B **52**
Shore La. Poole —2B **52**
Shore Rd. Poole —3H **67**
Short Clo. Poole —5C **38**
Shorts Clo. Burt —4G **43**
Shottsford Rd. Poole —2A **54**
Shrubb's Av. Lym —1G **51**
Sidney Gdns. Bourn —1C **40**
Silchester Clo. Bourn —2H **57**
Silver Bus. Pk. Christ —6B **44**
Silverdale. New M —5H **47**
Silverdale Clo. Broad —1E **35**
Silver St. Christ —1F **61**
Silver St. Hord —1D **48**
Silver Way. Christ —5G **45**
Silverwood Clo. Wim —1B **20**
Simmonds Clo. Poole —2B **54**
Singleton Dri. Bourn —3E **39**
Siskin Clo. Fern —2H **15**
Sixpenny Clo. Poole —6B **38**
Skinner St. Poole —6A **54**
Skipton Clo. Broad —3G **35**
Sky End La. Hord —3E **49**
Slade Clo. Hord —2E **49**
Slades Farm Rd. Bourn —4E **39**
Slade's La. Bourn —5E **39**
Sleepbrook Clo. Ver —3C **4**
Sleight La. Cor M —2C **18**
Slepe Cres. Poole —5B **38**
Slinn Rd. Christ —6A **44**
Slip Way. Poole —5H **53**

Slough La. Poole —1A **52**
Smithfield Pl. Bourn —4H **39**
Smithson Clo. Poole —5D **38**
Smithy La. New M —5F **29**
Smuggler's La. Wim —1F **13**
Smugglers La. N. Christ —3F **45**
Smugglers La. S. Christ —5F **45**
Smugglers View. New M —6C **46**
Smugglers Wood Rd. Christ
—4F **45**
Snail's La. Blash —1C **6**
Snowdon Rd. Bourn —3E **57**
Snowdrop Gdns. Christ —4D **44**
Soberton Rd. Bourn —6D **40**
Solent Av. Lym —2H **51**
Solent Clo. Lym —2H **51**
Solent Ct. Mil S —3C **64**
Solent Dri. New M —6G **47**
Solent Flats. Mil S —3E **65**
Solent Rd. Bourn —4E **61**
Solent Rd. Christ —3B **46**
Solent Rd. New M —6D **46**
Solent View. Bourn —4E **61**
Solent Way. Mil S —3F **65**
Solly Clo. Poole —6A **38**
Somerby Rd. Poole —1B **54**
Somerford Av. Christ —5D **44**
Somerford Bus. Pk. Christ —6C **44**
Somerford Rd. Christ —1A **62**
Somerford Way. Christ —6A **44**
Somerley Rd. Bourn —6A **40**
Somerley View. Ring —3C **6**
Somerset Rd. Bourn —2F **59**
Somerset Rd. Christ —6C **42**
Somerton Clo. New M —2B **48**
Somerville Rd. Bourn —4F **57**
Somerville Rd. Ring —3E **7**
Sonning Way. Bourn —3B **40**
Soper's La. Christ —1E **61**
Sopers La. Poole —4G **35**
Sopley Clo. New M —5D **46**
Sopwith Clo. Christ —1D **62**
Sopwith Cres. Wim —2C **20**
Sorrel Gdns. Broad —3F **35**
Sorrell Ct. Christ —5D **44**
Sorrell Way. Christ —5D **44**
Southampton Rd. Lym —5F **33**
Southampton Rd. Ring —4B **6**
South Av. New M —3H **47**
Southbourne Cliff Dri. Bourn
—4D **60**
Southbourne Coast Rd. Bourn
—4C **60**
Southbourne Gro. Bourn —3A **60**
Southbourne Overcliff Dri. Bourn
—4A **60**
Southbourne Promenade. Bourn
—4A **60**
Southbourne Rd. Bourn —1H **59**
Southbourne Rd. Lym —2E **51**
Southbrook Clo. Poole —3E **37**
Southcliffe Rd. Christ —1D **62**
Southcliffe Rd. New M —6D **46**
S. Cliff Rd. Bourn —5H **57**
Southcote Rd. Bourn —3B **58**
Southdown Way. W Moor —6D **8**
South Dri. St L —1F **17**
(off Oak Tree Farm Caravan Pk.)
Southern Av. W Moor —6E **9**
Southernhay Rd. Ver —3F **5**
Southern La. New M —5F **47**
Southern Oaks. New M —4F **47**
Southern Rd. Bourn —3A **60**
Southern Rd. Lym —2F **51**
Southey Rd. Christ —5B **44**
Southfield. Ring —5C **6**
Southfield M. Ring —5C **6**
South Gro. Lym —2H **51**
S. Haven Clo. Poole —4B **52**
Southill Av. Poole —1G **55**
Southill Gdns. Bourn —4A **40**
Southill Rd. Bourn —4A **40**
Southill Rd. Poole —1G **55**
S. Kinson Dri. Bourn —1C **38**
Southlands. Lym —3E **51**

Southlands Av. Bourn —3D **60**
Southlands Av. Cor M —5D **18**
Southlands Clo. Cor M —5D **18**
Southlawns Wlk. New M —4F **47**
Southlea Av. Bourn —2D **60**
South Pk. Rd. Poole —5C **38**
South Rd. Bourn —2E **59**
South Rd. Cor M —4D **18**
South Rd. Poole —5A **54**
South St. Lym —3E **51**
S. Sway La. Sway —3G **31**
S. View Pl. Bourn —4G **57**
S. View Rd. Christ —1E **61**
Southville Rd. Bourn —2H **59**
S. Western Cres. Poole —5F **55**
Southwick Pl. Bourn —6A **42**
Southwick Rd. Bourn —1A **60**
Southwood Av. Bourn —3A **60**
Southwood Av. Christ —4A **46**
Southwood Clo. Christ —4A **46**
Southwood Clo. Fern —3A **16**
Sovereign Bus. Pk. Poole —1H **53**
Sovereign Cen. Bourn —3E **59**
Sovereign Clo. Bourn —5F **41**
Sovereign Sq. Bourn —2E **59**
(off Royal Arc.)
Sparkford Clo. Bourn —5H **41**
Spartina Dri. Lym —5G **33**
Speedwell Dri. Christ —5D **44**
Spencer Ct. New M —3G **47**
Spencer Rd. Bourn —3C **58**
Spencer Rd. New M —2G **47**
Spencer Rd. Poole —1A **68**
Spetisbury Clo. Bourn —2B **40**
Spicer Ct. Bourn —4G **57**
(off Norwich Av.)
Spicer La. Bourn —6A **22**
(in two parts)
Spinacre. New M —5H **47**
Spindle Clo. Broad —3F **35**
Spindlewood Clo. New M —4G **47**
Spinners Clo. W Moor —6C **8**
Spinney Clo. St L —3H **9**
Spinneys La. Fern —4B **16**
Spinney, The. Ashy H —1B **10**
Spinney Way. New M —5G **29**
Spittlefields. Ring —4D **6**
Springbank Rd. Bourn —5F **41**
Springdale Av. Broad —6F **19**
Springdale Gro. Cor M —1D **34**
Springdale Rd. Cor M & Broad
—1D **34**
Springfield Av. Bourn —3E **61**
Springfield Av. Christ —3B **42**
Springfield Clo. Lym —2H **51**
Springfield Clo. Ver —4D **4**
Springfield Cres. Poole —3F **55**
Springfield Gdns. New M —3B **48**
Springfield Rd. Poole —2E **55**
Springfield Rd. Ver —4D **4**
Spring Gdns. Poole —2H **55**
Spring La. New M —3B **48**
Spring Rd. Bourn —2C **58**
Spring Rd. Lym —2H **51**
Springvale Av. Bourn —5F **41**
Springwater Clo. Bourn —2C **38**
Springwater Rd. Bourn —2C **38**
Spruce Clo. Poole —4E **35**
Spur Clo. Wim —3C **14**
Spurgeon Rd. Bourn —1H **59**
Spur Hill Av. Poole —4H **55**
Spur Rd. Poole —4H **55**
Square, The. Bourn —4H **57**
Square, The. Lym —2D **50**
Square, The. St L —1F **17**
(off Oak Tree Farm Caravan Pk.)
Square, The. Wim —4D **12**
Squirrels Clo. Christ —3B **42**
Squirrel Wlk. Ver —4D **4**
Stacey Clo. Poole —6G **37**
Stacey Gdns. Bourn —3F **41**
Stafford Rd. Bourn —4A **58**
Stag Bus. Pk. Ring —6C **6**
Stag Clo. New M —1E **47**
Stalbridge Dri. Fern —5B **16**

Stalbridge Rd. Poole —6G **35**
Stalham Rd. Poole —1B **56**
Stallards La. Ring —4B **6**
Stamford Rd. Bourn —2A **60**
Stanfield Clo. Poole —6H **37**
(in two parts)
Stanfield Rd. Bourn —5G **39**
Stanfield Rd. Fern —3A **16**
Stanfield Rd. Poole —6H **37**
Stanford Hill. Lym —2F **51**
Stanford Rise. Sway —1F **31**
Stanley Clo. Ver —4E **5**
Stanley Grn. Cres. Poole —2A **54**
Stanley Grn. Cres. Ind. Est. Poole
—2A **54**
Stanley Grn. Rd. Poole —2A **54**
Stanley Pearce Ho. Poole —4A **36**
Stanley Rd. Bourn —2C **58**
Stanley Rd. Christ —5A **46**
Stanley Rd. Lym —3H **51**
Stanley Rd. Poole —6B **54**
Stannington Clo. New M —3H **47**
Stanpit. Christ —1A **62**
Stanton Rd. Bourn —3E **39**
Stapehill Cres. Wim —4C **14**
Stapehill Rd. Wim —4E **15**
Stapehill Rd. Wim —6F **15**
Staple Clo. La. Poole —1A **54**
(in three parts)
Stapleford Av. Fern —3D **16**
Star La. Ring —4B **6**
Station App. Broad —1G **35**
Station Rd. Christ —6E **43**
Station Rd. Ham —6G **53**
Station Rd. New M —2G **47**
Station Rd. Park —3F **55**
Station Rd. Sway —1F **31**
Station Rd. Ver —2B **4**
Station Rd. W Moor —3B **8**
Station Rd. Wim —6F **13**
Station St. Lym —1H **51**
Station Ter. Wim —5F **13**
Stedman Rd. Bourn —1H **59**
Steepdene. Poole —4F **55**
Steeple Clo. Poole —2B **36**
Steepleton Rd. Broad —3A **36**
Stella Ct. Christ —6B **46**
Stem La. New M —2E **47**
Stem La. Ind. Est. New M —2E **47**
Stenhurst Rd. Poole —1C **54**
Stephen Langton Dri. Bourn
—6H **21**
Stephen's Wlk. Ring —4B **6**
(off Lyne's La.)
Sterte Av. Poole —3H **53**
Sterte Av. W. Poole —3H **53**
Sterte Clo. Poole —3A **54**
Sterte Rd. Poole —5A **54**
Stevenson Cres. Poole —4A **56**
Stevenson Rd. Bourn —4E **61**
Stevensons Clo. Wim —5E,**13**
Stewart Clo. Bourn —2C **58**
Stewart M. Bourn —2C **58**
Stewart Rd. Bourn —1A **58**
Stewarts Way. Fern —2C **16**
Stibbs Way. Brans —1E **27**
Stillmore Rd. Bourn —2H **37**
Stinsford Clo. Bourn —1B **40**
Stinsford Rd. Poole —5B **36**
Stirling Clo. New M —2H **47**
Stirling Rd. Bourn —6G **39**
Stirling Way. Christ —1D **62**
Stirrup Clo. Uptn —6H **34**
Stirrup Clo. Wim —3C **14**
Stoborough Dri. Broad —3F **35**
Stockbridge Clo. Poole —3F **37**
Stokes Av. Poole —3A **54**
Stoke Wood Rd. Bourn —1H **57**
Stonechat Clo. Fern —1H **15**
Stonechat Ct. Christ —6B **44**
Stonecrop Clo. Broad —3F **35**
Stone Gdns. Bourn —3G **41**
Stone La. Wim —3C **12**
Stone La. Ind. Est. Wim —3D **12**
Stoneleigh. Poole —1B **68**

Stoneleigh Av. Hord —1D 48
Stony La. Burt —2F 43
Stony La. S. Christ —1G 61
Stopples La. Hord —1D 48
Story La. Broad —1H 35
Stourbank Rd. Christ —1E 61
Stourcliffe Av. Bourn —3A 60
Stour Clo. Wim —5D 14
Stourcroft Dri. Christ —3B 42
Stourfield Rd. Bourn —3H 59
Stourpaine Rd. Poole —3B 36
Stour Pk. Caravan Pk. Bourn —5G 23
Stour Rd. Bourn —1C 58
Stour Rd. Christ —2D 60
Stourvale Av. Christ —5B 42
Stourvale Pl. Bourn —2H 59
Stourvale Rd. Bourn —2H 59
Stour View Gdns. Cor M —2E 19
Stour Wlk. Wim —6F 13
Stour Way. Christ —3B 42
Stourwood Av. Bourn —4A 60
Stourwood Rd. Bourn —3B 60
Stouts La. Brans —2D 26
Strand St. Poole —6A 54
Stratfield Pl. New M —2E 47
Stratford Pl. Lym —6F 33
Strathmore Dri. Ver —3E 5
Strathmore Rd. Bourn —1A 40
Stratton Rd. Bourn —1C 40
Strete Mt. Christ —6A 44
Stretton Ct. Poole —3F 55
Strides La. Ring —4A 6
Strode Gdns. St I —2D 10
Stroud Clo. Wim —3A 14
Strouden Av. Bourn —4B 40
Strouden Rd. Bourn —4A 40
Stroud Gdns. Christ —1A 62
Stroud La. Christ —1A 62
Stroud Pk. Av. Christ —1A 62
Struan Clo. Ashy H —1B 10
Struan Ct. Ashy H —1C 10
Struan Dri. Ashy H —1C 10
Struan Gdns. Ashy H —1B 10
Stuart Clo. Poole —6B 34
Stuart Rd. Christ —5B 46
Studland Dri. Mil S —2C 64
Studland Ho. Bourn —4B 58
Studland Rd. Bourn —6E 57
Studley Clo. Christ —5C 46
Studley Ct. New M —5D 46
Sturminster Rd. Bourn —1B 40
Suffolk Av. Christ —3D 42
Suffolk Clo. Wim —3C 14
Suffolk Rd. Bourn —4F 57
(in two parts)
Suffolk Rd. S. Bourn —3F 57
Summercroft Way. W Moor —4C 8
Summerfield Clo. Burt —3G 43
Summerfield Clo. Wim —5A 14
Summerfields. Bourn —6F 41
Summers Av. Bourn —5D 22
Summer's La. Burt —4H 43
Summertrees Ct. New M —1B 48
Sunbury Clo. Bourn —5C 22
Sunderland Dri. Christ —6D 44
Sundew Clo. New M —1B 48
Sundew Rd. Broad —3E 35
Sunningdale. Christ —1D 60
(off Fairway Dri.)
Sunningdale. Poole —4C 54
Sunningdale Cres. Bourn —1E 39
Sunningdale Gdns. Broad —6G 19
Sunnybank Dri. Wim —3B 14
Sunnybank Rd. Wim —3B 14
Sunnybank Way. Wim —3B 14
Sunnyfield Rd. New M —5G 47
Sunny Hill Ct. Poole —2H 55
Sunnyhill Rd. Bourn —2H 59
Sunny Hill Rd. Poole —2H 55
Sunnylands Av. Bourn —3D 60
Sunnymoor Rd. Bourn —4C 38
Sunnyside Pk. St I —2E 11
Sunnyside Rd. Poole —6H 37
Sunridge Clo. Poole —1C 56

Surrey Clo. Christ —3D 42
Surrey Gdns. Bourn —3E 57
Surrey Rd. Poole & Bourn —2C 56
Surrey Rd. S. Bourn —3E 57
Sussex Clo. Bourn —6C 24
Sutherland Av. Broad —6E 19
Sutton Clo. Poole —3F 37
Sutton Rd. Bourn —4B 40
Swallow Clo. Poole —5F 35
Swallow Dri. Mil S —3E 65
Swallow Way. Wim —1A 14
Swan Mead. High —5E 7
Swanmore Rd. Bourn —1H 59
Swansbury Dri. Bourn —3H 41
Sway Gdns. Bourn —3D 40
Sway Rd. Lym —6A 32
Sway Rd. New M —5G 29
Sweep, The. Ring —4B 6
Swift Clo. Poole —5F 35
Swordfish Dri. Christ —6D 44
Sycamore Clo. Christ —5B 42
Sycamore Clo. Mil S —2C 64
Sycamore Clo. Poole —4F 35
Sycamore Ct. Ring —1E 7
Sycamore Rd. Hord —1D 48
Sydling Clo. Poole —3F 37
Sydney Rd. Broad —2G 35
Sydney Rd. Christ —4C 42
Sylmor Gdns. Bourn —3A 40
Sylvan Clo. Hord —3F 49
Sylvan Clo. St L —3H 9
Sylvan Rd. Poole —1F 55
Symes Rd. Poole —3E 53

Tadden Wlk. Broad —3F 35
Tait Clo. Poole —6C 36
Talbot Av. Bourn —5F 39
Talbot Ct. Bourn —4H 39
Talbot Dri. Christ —3H 45
Talbot Dri. Poole —5D 38
Talbot Hill Rd. Bourn —5F 39
Talbot Meadows. Poole —5D 38
Talbot M. Bourn —4D 38
Talbot Rise. Bourn —3E 39
Talbot Rd. Bourn —5F 39
Tamar Clo. Poole —3C 36
Tamworth Rd. Bourn —2F 59
Tanglewood Lodge. Poole —5F 35
Tangmere Clo. Christ —1D 62
Tangmere Pl. Poole —6C 36
Tan Howse Clo. Bourn —5H 41
Tapper Ct. Wim —5G 13
Tarn Dri. Poole —4F 35
Tarrant Clo. Poole —3C 36
Tarrant Rd. Bourn —2B 40
Tasman Clo. Christ —5D 42
Tatnam La. Poole —3A 54
Tatnam Rd. Poole —3A 54
Taverner Clo. Poole —6B 54
Taylors Bldgs. Poole —6A 54
Teak Ho., The. Poole —1D 68
Teasel Way. W Moor —6C 8
Tedder Clo. Bourn —2D 38
Tedder Gdns. Bourn —2D 38
Tedder Rd. Bourn —2D 38
Telford Rd. Wim —1G 15
Templer Clo. Bourn —4B 38
Tennyson Rd. Bourn —3H 39
Tennyson Rd. Poole —4E 55
Tennyson Rd. Wim —3E 13
Tensing Rd. Christ —5A 44
Terence Av. Poole —4A 36
Terence Rd. Cor M —6C 18
Tern Ct. Bourn —1B 60
Terrace Rd. Bourn —4G 57
Terrington Av. Christ —4G 45
Thames All. Bourn —6H 53
(off Thames M.)
Thames Clo. Fern —3E 17
Thames M. Bourn —6H 53
Thames St. Poole —6H 53
Theobald Rd. Hurn —3G 25
(off Brackley Clo.)
Thetchers Clo. New M —6H 29

Thetford Rd. Poole —2B 56
Third Marine Av. New M —6G 47
Thistlebarrow Rd. Bourn —2B 40
Thoresby Ct. New M —2E 47
Thornbury Rd. Bourn —3E 61
Thorncombe Clo. Bourn —1B 40
Thorncombe Clo. Poole —3C 36
Thorne Way. T Leg —1F 9
Thornfield Dri. Christ —4H 45
Thornham Rd. New M —2B 48
Thornley Rd. Bourn —1F 39
Thorn Rd. Poole —2B 36
Three Acre Clo. New M —5E 47
Three Acre Dri. New M —5F 47
Three Cross Rd. W Moor —1C 8
Throop Clo. Bourn —3G 41
Throop Rd. Bourn —6D 24
Throopside Av. Bourn —1D 40
Thrush Rd. Poole —4G 37
Thursby Rd. Christ —3H 45
Thwaite Rd. Poole —2D 56
Tiffany Clo. Hord —1D 48
Tilburg Rd. Christ —6H 43
Timothy Clo. Bourn —6F 23
Tincleton Gdns. Bourn —1B 40
Tins, The. Lym —1G 51
Tiptoe Rd. New M —2G 29
Tithe Barn. Lym —6G 33
Todber Clo. Bourn —2H 37
Tollard Clo. Poole —5A 38
Tollerford Rd. Poole —3B 36
Tolpuddle Gdns. Bourn —1B 40
Tolstoi Rd. Poole —1E 55
Tonge Rd. Bourn —5D 22
Top La. Ring —4C 6
Torbay Rd. Poole —4G 55
Totlan Ct. Mil S —3C 64
Totmel Rd. Poole —3E 37
Tourney Rd. Bourn —5H 21
Tower La. Wim —3F 13
Tower Pk. Poole —4F 37
Tower Rd. Bourn —2E 59
Tower Rd. Poole —5D 56
Tower Rd. W. Poole —6C 56
Towers Farm. Cor M —4D 18
Towers Way. Cor M —4D 18
Towngate Bri. Poole —5A 54
Townsend Clo. Bourn —5D 22
Townsville Rd. Bourn —3B 40
Tozer Clo. Bourn —3B 38
Trafalgar Ct. Christ —2B 62
Trafalgar Rd. Bourn —6H 39
Tranmere Clo. Lym —3H 51
Travellers Rest Rd. T Leg —2A 8
Treebys Clo. Burt —4H 43
Tree Hamlets. Poole —2C 52
Treeside. Christ —3F 45
Trefoil Way. Christ —5E 45
Tregonwell Rd. Bourn —4G 57
Trentham Av. Bourn —5H 41
Trentham Clo. Bourn —5H 41
Trent Way. Fern —3E 17
Tresillian Clo. Christ —3B 46
Tresillian Way. Christ —3B 46
Triangle, The. Bourn —4G 57
Triangle, The. New M —5C 46
Tricketts La. Fern —3D 16
Trigon Rd. Poole —6B 36
Tringham Ho. Bourn —5H 41
Trinidad Cres. Poole —5G 37
Trinidad Ho. Poole —5G 37
Trinity Rd. Bourn —3A 58
Troak Clo. Christ —5A 44
Troon Rd. Broad —6G 19
Trotters La. Wim —3B 14
Truman Rd. Bourn —5D 22
Trumpeters Ct. Wim —4D 12
Truscott Av. Bourn —6A 40
Tuckers La. Poole —6F 53
Tuck's Clo. Brans —2C 26
Tuckton Clo. Bourn —3B 60
Tuckton Rd. Bourn —3B 60
Tudor Ct. Poole —1C 54
Tudor Rd. Broad —1H 35
Turbary Clo. Poole —5H 37

Turbary Ct. Poole —5C 34
Turbary Pk. Av. Bourn —2B 38
Turbary Rd. Fern —2D 16
Turbary Rd. Poole —6H 37
Turks La. Poole —6E 55
Turlin Rd. Poole —3C 52
Turners Farm Cres. Hord —3E 49
Turnworth Clo. Broad —2A 36
Tweedale Rd. Bourn —2C 40
Tweed La. Bold —2F 33
Twemlow Av. Poole —5D 54
Twin Oaks Clo. Broad —2G 35
Twyford Clo. Bourn —3D 40
Twyford Way. Poole —3E 37
Twynham Av. Christ —6E 43
Twynham Rd. Bourn —4C 60
Tylers Clo. Lym —6F 33
Tyndale Cres. Bourn —1C 40
Tyneham Av. Poole —5G 37
Tyrrell Gdns. Bourn —3G 41
Tyrrells Ct. Brans —2D 26
Tytherley Grn. Bourn —3D 40

Uddens Dri. Wim —1D 14
Uddens Trading Est. Wim —3E 15
Ullswater Rd. Wim —1A 20
Undercliff Dri. Bourn —5A 58
Undercliff Rd. Bourn —4E 59
Undershore. Lym —5G 33
Underwood Clo. Poole —4H 35
Uplands Av. New M —5G 47
Uplands Clo. W Moor —1E 17
Uplands Rd. Bourn —4B 40
Uplands Rd. W Moor —1E 17
Uplyme Clo. Poole —3E 37
Up. Common Rd. Penn —1B 50
Up. Golf Links Rd. Broad —6H 19
Up. Gordon Rd. Christ —4A 46
Up. Hinton Rd. Bourn —4H 57
Up. Norwich Rd. Bourn —4G 57
Upper Rd. Poole —6F 37
Up. Terrace Rd. Bourn —4G 57
Uppleby Rd. Poole —2G 55
(in two parts)
Upton Clo. Poole —6B 34
Upton Ct. Uptn —6C 34
Upton Heath Est. Poole —6D 34
Upton Rd. Poole —6C 34
Upton Way. Broad —2E 35
Upwey Av. Poole —4E 53
Utrecht Ct. Christ —6H 43

Vaggs La. Hord —4B 30
Vale Clo. Poole —3A 56
Valencia Clo. Christ —1B 42
Vale Rd. Bourn —3D 58
Vale Rd. Poole —3A 56
Valette Rd. Bourn —1A 40
Valiant Way. Christ —6D 44
Valley Clo. Christ —2C 42
Valley Rd. Bourn —2F 41
Valley View. Poole —6D 38
Vallis Clo. Poole —6B 54
Vanguard Rd. Bourn —4E 41
Vanguard Rd. Poole —5A 54
Vecta Clo. Christ —1E 63
Vectis Rd. New M —6D 46
Velvet Lawn Rd. New M —1F 47
Venator Pl. Wim —3E 13
Venning Av. Bourn —6A 22
Ventry Clo. Poole —3B 56
Ventura Pl. Poole —1D 52
Verity Cres. Poole —4D 36
Vernalls Clo. Bourn —5F 23
Vernalls Gdns. Bourn —5F 23
Verne Rd. Ver —4E 5
Verney Clo. Bourn —2D 38
Verney Rd. Bourn —2C 38
Verno La. Christ —4E 45
Verona Av. Bourn —2B 60
Verulam Pl. Bourn —4H 57
Verulam Rd. Bourn —3D 54
Verwood Cres. Bourn —3E 61

Verwood Ind. Est. Ver —3F **5**
Verwood Mnr. Ct. Ver —3D **4**
Verwood Rd. Ashy —1F **11**
Verwood Rd. T Leg —2A **8**
Vetch Clo. Christ —5D **44**
Vicarage Gdns. Hord —2E **49**
Vicarage La. Hord —2E **49**
Vicarage Rd. Bourn —3G **39**
Vicarage Rd. Poole —2A **54**
Vicarage Rd. Ver —3D **4**
Vicarage Way. Burt —3H **43**
Vickers Clo. Bourn —3H **41**
Vickery Way. Christ —5H **43**
Victoria Av. Bourn —4G **39**
Victoria Clo. Cor M —1D **34**
Victoria Cres. Poole —1H **55**
Victoria Gdns. Fern —3B **16**
Victoria Gdns. Ring —5C **6**
Victoria Pk. Rd. Bourn —4G **39**
Victoria Pl. Bourn —2C **58**
Victoria Pl. Lym —3G **51**
Victoria Pl. Wim —4D **12**
Victoria Rd. Bourn —2C **58**
Victoria Rd. Christ —2A **62**
Victoria Rd. Fern —3B **16**
Victoria Rd. Mil S —3B **64**
Victoria Rd. Poole —2G **55**
Victoria Rd. Wim —4D **12**
Victory Clo. T Leg —1F **9**
View Point Ct. Poole —1E **55**
Viewside Clo. Cor M —6C **18**
Viking Clo. Bourn —3E **61**
Viking Way. Bourn —3E **61**
Viking Way. Christ —2C **62**
Village Hall La. T Leg —1A **8**
Villette Clo. Christ —4E **43**
Vince Clo. Bourn —6D **22**
Vincent Clo. New M —3G **47**
Vincent Rd. New M —2F **47**
Vine Clo. Bourn —6G **41**
Vine Farm Clo. Poole —5B **38**
Vine Farm Rd. Poole —5D **38**
Vinegar Hill. Mil S —2D **64**
Vine Hill. Wim —4A **12**
Vineries Clo. Wim —3H **13**
Vineries, The. Wim —4H **13**
Vinery, The. New M —3H **47**
Viney Rd. Lym —2H **51**
Vinneys Clo. Burt —3G **43**
Violet Farm Clo. Cor M —3D **18**
Violet La. New M —1G **47**
Virginia Clo. Poole —6G **37**
Viscount Clo. Bourn —6H **21**
(in two parts)
Viscount Dri. Christ —6D **44**
Viscount Wlk. Bourn —6G **21**
Vitre Gdns. Lym —3G **51**
Vixen Wlk. New M —5H **29**
Vulcan Way. Christ —6D **44**

Wagtail Dri. New M —3F **47**
Wainsford Clo. Lym —2D **50**
(in two parts)
Wainsford Rd. Evtn —3A **50**
Wakefield Av. Bourn —6G **23**
Wakely Gdns. Bourn —6C **22**
Wakely Rd. Bourn —6D **22**
Walcheren Pl. Poole —4C **52**
Walcott Av. Christ —4D **42**
Walditch Gdns. Poole —3C **36**
Waldren Clo. Poole —5B **54**
Walford Clo. Wim —3E **13**
Walford Gdns. Wim —3D **12**
Walhampton Hill. Lym —6H **33**
Walkford La. New M —3D **46**
Walkford Rd. Christ —4B **46**
Walkford Way. Christ —4B **46**
Walkwood Av. Bourn —5H **41**
Wallace Rd. Broad —2G **35**
Walliscott Rd. Bourn —4C **38**
Wallisdown Heights. Bourn —4B **38**
Wallisdown Rd. Bourn & Poole
—3H **37**
Wallis Rd. Bourn —4D **38**

Walnut Clo. New M —2F **47**
Walpole Rd. Bourn —2D **58**
Walsford Rd. Bourn —2E **57**
Walsingham Dene. Bourn —5F **41**
Waltham Rd. Bourn —6H **41**
Walton Rd. Bourn —3E **39**
Walton Rd. Poole —1E **55**
Wanstead Clo. Ring —2D **6**
Warbler Clo. Poole —5B **34**
Warborne La. Lym —3H **33**
Warburton Rd. Poole —5C **36**
Wareham Ct. Bourn —1H **59**
Wareham Rd. Cor M —2A **34**
Warland Way. Cor M —4E **19**
Warmwell Clo. Bourn —2B **40**
Warmwell Clo. Poole —3D **36**
Warnford Rd. Bourn —6H **41**
Warren Av. Christ —2B **62**
Warren Clo. Ring —2F **11**
Warren Dri. Bourn —2F **11**
Warren Edge Clo. Bourn —4D **60**
Warren Edge Rd. Bourn —4D **60**
Warren La. Ring —2F **11**
Warren Pk. Mil S —1A **64**
Warren Rd. Bourn —5D **56**
Warren Rd. Poole —3H **55**
Warren Wlk. Fern —2H **15**
Warwick Av. New M —2H **47**
Warwick La. Ver —1A **4**
Warwick Pl. Bourn —2G **59**
Warwick Rd. Bourn —2G **59**
Warwick Rd. Poole —4G **55**
Washington Av. Bourn —1D **58**
Watcombe Rd. Bourn —2B **60**
Waterditch Rd. Brans —2B **44**
Waterford Clo. Lym —2H **51**
Waterford Clo. Poole —5E **55**
Waterford Gdns. Christ —6A **46**
Waterford La. Lym —2H **51**
Waterford Pl. Christ —6A **46**
Waterford Rd. Christ —5B **46**
Waterford Rd. New M —2A **48**
Water La. Bourn —6B **42**
Waterloo Rd. Bourn —6H **39**
Waterloo Rd. Cor M —5B **18**
Waterloo Rd. Lym —1H **51**
Waterloo Rd. Poole —6H **35**
Waterloo Way. Ring —5C **6**
Watermead. Christ —2E **61**
Watermill Rd. Christ —5E **43**
Watership Dri. Ring —5F **7**
Waterside. Christ —3B **62**
Waterside Clo. Ring —2D **6**
Water Tower Rd. Broad —1A **36**
Watery La. Christ —4C **44**
Watery La. Poole —6A **34**
Watford Rd. New M —2A **48**
Watkin Rd. Bourn —3F **59**
Watton Clo. Bourn —3G **41**
Wavell Av. Poole —4G **35**
Wavell Rd. Bourn —1D **38**
Wavendon Av. New M —5E **47**
Waverley Cres. Poole —2B **54**
Waverley Rd. Bourn —3B **58**
Waverley Rd. New M —3H **47**
Wayground Rd. Cor M —2E **19**
Wayman Rd. Cor M —5E **19**
Wayne Rd. Poole —1F **55**
Wayside Clo. Mil S —2D **64**
Wayside Rd. Bourn —3C **60**
Wayside Rd. St L —6A **10**
Waytown Clo. Poole —4B **36**
Weavers Clo. W Moor —6C **8**
Webbs Clo. Ashy H —1H **9**
Webbs Way. Ashy H —1A **10**
Webbs Way. Bourn —4B **38**
Webster Rd. Bourn —2A **40**
Wedgwood Dri. Poole —5E **55**
Wedgwood Gdns. Brans —2E **27**
Weldon Av. Bourn —6A **22**
Welland Rd. Wim —5F **13**
Well Clo. New M —3F **47**
Wellesley Av. Christ —6D **44**
Wellington Av. Christ —6E **45**
Wellington Ct. Bourn —4F **57**

Wellington Ct. New M —2G **47**
Wellington Rd. Bourn —1A **58**
Wellington Rd. Poole —4G **55**
Well La. Poole —3A **54**
Wendover Clo. New M —4F **47**
*Wendys Rd. Fern —6D **16***
(off Lone Pine Caravan Pk.)
Wentwood Gdns. New M —3B **48**
Wentworth Av. Bourn —3G **59**
Wentworth Clo. Bourn —4G **59**
Wentworth Dri. Broad —6G **19**
Wentworth Dri. Christ —1D **60**
Wescott Way. Bourn —1A **38**
Wesley Rd. Poole —2G **55**
Wesley Rd. Wim —4F **13**
Wessex Av. New M —3G **47**
Wessex Clo. Christ —6E **45**
Wessex Est. Ring —3E **7**
Wessex Fields. Bourn —4H **41**
Wessex Rd. Poole —4E **55**
Wessex Rd. Ring —3D **6**
Wessex Trade Cen. Poole —6F **37**
Wessex Way. Bourn —3D **56**
West Av. T Leg —2A **8**
Westbeams Rd. Sway —1F **31**
W. Borough. Wim —3D **12**
Westbourne Arc. Bourn —4D **56**
Westbourne Clo. Bourn —4E **57**
Westbourne Pk. Rd. Bourn —5D **56**
Westbury Clo. Brans —4C **26**
Westbury Clo. Christ —4F **45**
Westbury Clo. New M —5G **47**
Westbury Rd. Ring —4D **6**
W. Butts St. Poole —1H **55**
Westby Rd. Bourn —3E **59**
W. Cliff Gdns. Bourn —5G **57**
W. Cliff Promenade. Bourn —5F **57**
(in two parts)
W. Cliff Rd. Bourn —5E **57**
West Clo. Bourn —3E **61**
West Clo. Lym —3D **50**
West Clo. Ver —2B **4**
Westcroft Pde. New M —3G **47**
Westcroft Pk. Broad —1A **36**
Westdown Rd. Bourn —6C **22**
*West Dri. St L —1F **17***
(off Oak Tree Farm Caravan Pk.)
Westerham Rd. Bourn —4D **56**
Western Av. Bourn —6F **23**
Western Av. New M —5D **46**
Western Av. Poole —4A **56**
Western Clo. Bourn —6F **23**
Western Rd. Lym —1F **51**
Western Rd. Poole —1B **68**
Westfield Clo. Wim —4D **12**
Westfield Gdns. Christ —4D **44**
Westfield Rd. Bourn —3C **60**
Westfield Rd. Lym —3H **51**
Westgate Pk. Bourn —4D **56**
Westham Clo. Poole —2C **36**
West Hayes. Lym —2H **51**
Westheath Rd. Broad —1H **35**
W. Hill Pl. Bourn —4G **57**
W. Hill Rd. Bourn —4G **57**
W. Howe Clo. Bourn —1C **38**
W. Howe Ind. Est. Bourn —2A **38**
Westlands. Brans —3C **26**
West La. Evtn —4A **50**
Westminster Ct. New M —6F **47**
Westminster Rd. Mil S —3A **64**
Westminster Rd. Poole —6D **56**
Westminster Rd. E. Poole —6D **56**
W. Moors Rd. Fern —2B **16**
W. Moors Rd. T Leg —2A **8**
W. Moors Rd. W Moor —3B **8**
Weston Dri. Bourn —4B **58**
Weston Rd. Wim —2H **13**
Westons La. Poole —5A **54**
W. Overcliff Dri. Bourn —5E **57**
Westover La. Ring —1F **11**
Westover Rd. Bourn —4H **57**
Westover Rd. Mil S —3D **64**
*W. Quay M. Poole —6H **53***
(off W. Quay Rd.)
W. Quay Rd. Poole —5H **53**

West Rd. Bourn —2G **59**
West Rd. Brans —2C **26**
West Rd. Mil S —2A **64**
West Row. Wim —5D **12**
*West Sta. Ter. Bourn —4F **57***
(off Queens Rd.)
West St. Poole —6H **53**
West St. Ring —4A **6**
West St. Wim —4D **12**
W. Undercliff Promenade. Bourn
—6F **57**
Westview Rd. Christ —1A **62**
W. View Rd. Poole —3A **54**
West Way. Bourn —3B **40**
West Way. Broad —3B **35**
West Way. Lym —3E **51**
West Way. Clo. Bourn —4B **40**
Westwood Av. Fern —3A **16**
Westwoods Pk. New M —6D **28**
Wetherby Clo. Broad —3G **35**
Weyman's Av. Bourn —5E **23**
Weyman's Dri. Bourn —5E **23**
Weymouth Rd. Poole —2G **55**
Wharf Clo. Poole —1A **56**
Wharfdale Rd. Bourn —3E **57**
Wharfdale Rd. Poole —1H **55**
Wharncliffe Gdns. Christ —6A **46**
Wharncliffe Rd. Bourn —3D **58**
Wharncliffe Rd. Christ —6H **45**
Whatleigh Clo. Poole —6A **54**
Wheaton Rd. Bourn —2G **59**
Wheeler's La. Bourn —5G **21**
Whincroft Clo. Fern —2C **16**
Whincroft Dri. Fern —2C **16**
Whitaker Cres. Lym —2E **51**
Whitby Av. Broad —3F **35**
Whitby Clo. Christ —1B **42**
Whitby Ct. Mil S —3B **64**
Whitby Cres. Broad —3F **35**
Whitby Rd. Mil S —3B **64**
Whitchurch Av. Broad —2A **36**
White Barn Cres. Hord —2E **49**
Whitebeam Way. Ver —4F **5**
Whitecliff Cres. Poole —5E **55**
Whitecliff Rd. Poole —5D **54**
White Clo. Poole —6E **37**
Whitecross Clo. Poole —2C **36**
White Farm Clo. Bourn —5F **39**
Whitefield Rd. New M —2G **47**
Whitefield Rd. Poole —5E **55**
Whitehall. Christ —2F **61**
Whitehayes Clo. Burt —3H **43**
Whitehayes Rd. Burt —3G **43**
White Horse Dri. Poole —2A **54**
Whitehorses. New M —6E **47**
Whitehouse Rd. Wim —1B **20**
White Knights. New M —6F **47**
Whitelegg Way. Bourn —6G **23**
Whiteways. Wim —3G **13**
Whitfield Pk. Ring —2D **10**
Whitley Way. New M —6H **29**
Whitsbury Clo. Bourn —3D **40**
Whittle Rd. Wim —2F **15**
Whittles Way. Poole —5H **53**
Wick 1 Ind. Est. New M —3E **47**
Wick 2 Ind. Est. New M —3E **47**
Wick Clo. New M —3E **47**
Wick Dri. New M —3E **47**
Wicket Rd. Bourn —6E **23**
Wickfield Av. Christ —1F **61**
Wickfield Clo. Christ —1F **61**
Wickham Dri. Cor M —1D **34**
Wickham Rd. Bourn —2G **59**
Wick La. Bourn —2D **60**
Wick La. Christ —2F **61**
Wicklea Rd. Bourn —3F **61**
Wickmeads Rd. Bourn —2E **61**
Widbury Rd. Lym —2E **51**
Widden Clo. Sway —1F **31**
Widdicombe Av. Poole —5A **56**
Widget Clo. Bourn —3D **38**
Widworthy Dri. Broad —6F **19**
Wight Wlk. W Parl —1G **23**
Wilderton Rd. Poole —4B **56**

Wilderton Rd. W. Poole —3C 56
Wildfell Clo. Christ —4E 43
Wildown Gdns. Bourn —4D 60
Wildown Rd. Bourn —4E 61
Wilfred Rd. Bourn —3F 59
Wilkinson Dri. Bourn —3G 41
Wilkins Way. Poole —5H 53
Willett Rd. Ashtn —1F 19
William Clo. Christ —3A 46
William Ct. Christ —6B 46
William Rd. Bourn —6F 41
William Rd. Lym —6G 33
Williams Ind. Pk. New M —3E 47
Willis Way. Poole —1H 53
Willow Clo. Bourn —2D 56
Willow Clo. Poole —2D 52
Willow Clo. St L —3H 9
Willowdene Clo. New M —2A 48
Willow Dri. Christ —2E 61
Willow Dri. Poole —3B 56
Willow Dri. Wim —3C 14
Willow Mead. Bourn —1D 40
Willow Pk. Poole —4D 54
Willows, The. New M —5H 47
Willow Tree Rise. Bourn —2D 38
Willow Way. Christ —2E 61
Willow Way. Fern —1B 16
Wills Clo. Cor M —1D 34
Wills Rd. Poole —3B 56
Willwood Clo. Poole —2C 36
Wilmur Cres. Poole —1C 54
Wilson Rd. Bourn —1D 58
Wilson Rd. Poole —3G 55
Wilton Clo. Christ —4B 42
Wilton Gdns. New M —2F 47
Wilton Rd. Bourn —2F 59
Wiltshire Gdns. Brans —3B 26
Wiltshire Rd. Brans —3B 26
Wilverley Av. Bourn —3F 41
Wilverley Clo. Lym —3D 50
Wilverley Rd. Christ —6C 44
Wilverley Rd. New M —1F 29
Wimborne Ho. Bourn —1H 57
Wimborne Minster By-Pass. Wim —6B 12
Wimborne Rd. Bourn —3H 57
Wimborne Rd. Bourn —5B 22 (Kinson)
Wimborne Rd. Cole —3F 13
Wimborne Rd. Poole —6A 36
Wimborne Rd. Walf —3D 12
Wimborne Rd. E. Fern —3G 15
Wimborne Rd. W. Wim —5A 14
Winchester Rd. New M —6A 30
Wincombe Clo. Fern —6B 16
Wincombe Dri. Fern —5B 16
Windermere Rd. Bourn —6C 44
Windgreen Est. Cor M —4E 19
Windham Rd. Bourn —2C 58

Windmill Clo. Mil S —2D 64
Windmill Clo. Ring —3F 11
Windmill La. Ring —3F 11
Windsor Clo. Hord —1C 48
Windsor Clo. St I —3B 10
Windsor Rd. Bourn —3E 59
Windsor Rd. Christ —5C 42
Windsor Rd. Poole —4F 55
Winfrith Cres. Poole —5A 38
Wingfield Av. Christ —4F 45
Wingfield Av. Poole —1B 54
Wingfield Ct. Bourn —4C 58
Winifred Rd. Poole —2C 54
Winkton Clo. Burt —2G 43
Winkton Grn. Wink —1G 43
Winnards Clo. W Parl —1G 23
Winsford Clo. Christ —4F 45
Winsley Av. Bourn —3A 60
Winspit Clo. Poole —4E 53
Winston Av. Poole —1B 56
Winston Ct. Christ —6E 43
Winston Gdns. Poole —1C 56
Winston Rd. Bourn —2A 40
Winston Way. Ring —3D 6
Winterbourne Clo. Poole —2B 54
Winterbourne Rd. Poole —2B 54
Winterhayes Clo. Poole —2B 36
Winton Clo. Lym —2H 51
Winton Way. New M —6H 29
Wishart Gdns. Bourn —6B 24
Wisteria Dri. Ver —5G 5
Wisteria Ho. Bourn —1H 39
Witchampton Rd. Broad —3F 35
Withermoor Rd. Bourn —5G 39
Withingham Rd. Poole —4B 56
Woking Rd. Poole —3G 55
Wolfe Clo. Christ —6A 44
Wollaston Rd. Bourn —4D 60
Wollaton Cres. Fern —6A 16
Wollaton Rd. Fern —6A 16
Wollstonecraft Rd. Bourn —4F 59
Wolseley Rd. Poole —1H 55
Wolsey Way. Mil S —2D 64
Wolterton Rd. Poole —1C 56
Wolverton Rd. Bourn —2F 59
Wonderholme Pde. Bourn —3D 38
Woodacre Gdns. Fern —5C 16
Woodbury Av. Bourn —3E 41
Woodbury Clo. Christ —2C 42
Woodcock La. Hord —2E 49
Woodcocks Cres. Bourn —5G 41
Wood Cote Dri. Poole —1B 52
Woodend Rd. Bourn —5G 39
Woodend Rd. Crow —6G 7
Woodfield Gdns. Christ —4F 45
Woodfield Rd. Bourn —6G 22
Woodford Clo. Ring —4E 7
Woodford Rd. Bourn —3C 58
Woodgreen Dri. Poole —1H 37
Woodhayes Av. Christ —3G 45

Woodland Av. Bourn —3G 59
Woodland Ct. Cor M —1D 34
Woodlands Av. Poole —4F 53
Woodlands Caravan Pk. Hord —2E 49
Woodlands Clo. Brans —3C 26
Woodlands Cres. Poole —4F 53
Woodlands Rd. New M —6E 47
Woodlands Way. St I —3B 10
Woodland View. Mil S —1A 64
Woodland Wlk. Bourn —3G 59
Woodland Wlk. Fern —2C 16
Woodland Way. Christ —5F 45
Woodland Way. Mil S —3C 64
Woodland Way. New M —5H 29
Wood La. Bourn —5A 22
Wood La. Mil S —3C 64
Wood Lawn Clo. New M —5F 47
Woodleaze Clo. Broad —5H 19
Woodley Gdns. Lym —6F 33
Woodlinken Clo. Ver —5F 5
Woodlinken Dri. Ver —5F 5
Woodlinken Way. Ver —5G 5
Woodpecker Clo. Ver —4D 4
Woodpecker Dri. Poole —5E 35
Woodside Av. Lym —4G 51
Woodside Clo. Fern —3C 16
Woodside Clo. Lym —3G 51
Woodside La. Lym —3G 51
Woodside Rd. Bourn —3H 59
Woodside Rd. Fern —2C 16
Woodside Rd. Poole —4G 55
Woodside Rd. W Moor —3B 8
Woodstock Clo. Poole —5F 55
Woodstock La. Ring —4C 6
Woodstock Rd. Burt —3H 43
Woodstock Rd. Poole —5E 55
Woods View Rd. Bourn —5F 39
Woodvale Gdns. New M —1A 48
Wood View. Wim —1A 14
Woolmer La. Blash —1C 6
Wool Rd. Poole —5F 37
Woolsbridge Rd. Ashy H —1B 10
Woolsbridge Small Bus. Cen. T Leg —1F 9
Woolslope Clo. W Moor —6C 8
Woolslope Gdns. W Moor —6D 8
Woolslope Rd. W Moor —6C 8
Woolven Clo. Poole —2E 55
Wootton Farm Rd. New M —1E 29
Wootton Gdns. Bourn —4A 58
Wootton Mt. Bourn —4A 58
Wootton Rd. Tip —3B 30
Wootton Rough. New M —3H 29
Worbarrow Gdns. Poole —5G 37
Worcester Pl. Lym —3H 51
Wordsworth Av. Bourn —4E 41
Worgret Rd. Poole —6B 36
Worley Way. Fern —6D 16
(off Lone Pine Caravan Pk.)

Worrell Dri. Poole —5G 37
Worthington Cres. Poole —4E 55
Worthy Rd. New M —2G 47
Wortley Rd. Christ —6A 46
Wraxall Clo. Poole —4B 36
Wren Clo. Christ —2D 62
Wren Clo. High —5E 7
Wren Clo. New M —3F 47
Wren Cres. Poole —2C 56
Wroxham Rd. Poole —2B 56
Wyatts Clo. Cor M —5D 18
Wyatts La. Cor M —5C 18
Wychwood Clo. Bourn —3G 57
Wychwood Dri. Bourn —2H 57
Wycliffe Rd. Bourn —5H 39
Wyelands Av. Wim —4D 14
Wykeham Clo. Poole —5C 36
Wykeham Pl. Lym —2G 51
Wyncombe Rd. Bourn —2H 59
Wyndham Clo. Christ —3B 46
Wyndham Rd. Christ —3B 46
Wyndham Rd. Poole —3B 56
Wynford Rd. Bourn —1A 40
Wynford Rd. Poole —3G 55
Wynne Clo. Broad —1F 35
Wynter Clo. Bourn —5F 41
Wyvern Clo. Poole —6H 37

Yaldhurst La. Lym —1D 50
Yarmouth Clo. Poole —2C 56
Yarrell Mead. Lym —1D 50
Yarrell's Clo. Poole —1C 52
Yarrells Dri. Poole —6B 34
Yarrells La. Poole —1C 52
Yarrow Clo. Christ —5D 44
Yarrow Rd. Poole —6E 37
Yeatminster Rd. Poole —3D 36
Yelverton Rd. Bourn —4H 57
Yeomans Ind. Pk. Bourn —3E 41
Yeomans Rd. Bourn —3D 40
Yeomans Way. Bourn —3E 41
Yeovilton Clo. Evtn —4A 50
Yew La. New M —1A 48
Yew Tree Clo. Wim —4F 13
Yew Tree Ct. New M —4H 47
York Av. New M —2H 47
York Clo. Broad —3G 35
York Clo. Christ —6D 42
York Pl. Bourn —2G 59
York Pl. New M —2H 47
York Rd. Bourn —3B 58
York Rd. Broad —4G 35
Youngs Rd. Bourn —6C 22

Zamek Clo. Bourn —6C 22
Zinnia Clo. Bourn —3G 39

Every possible care has been taken to ensure that the information given in this publication is accurate and whilst the publishers would be grateful to learn of any errors, they regret they cannot accept any responsibility for loss thereby caused.

The representation on the maps of a road, track or footpath is no evidence of the existence of a right of way.

Copyright of Geographers' A-Z Map Co. Ltd.

No reproduction by any method whatsoever of any part of this publication is permitted without the prior consent of the copyright owners.